The Ultimate Guide to:
SOY CANDLE MAKING

From Hobby Enthusiasts to Business Professionals

Jameel D. Nolan

The author hopes you enjoy the projects discussed in this book. While we believe the projects to be safe and fun if proper safety precautions are followed, all such projects are done at the reader's sole risk. The author cannot accept any responsibility or liability for any damages, loss, or injury arising from use, misuse, or misconception of the information provided in this book. In addition, business and legal information provided in this book is for reference purposes only, and is not intended to be legal or business advice. You should always consult a legal professional regarding the laws that may apply to your business.

Exterior Illustrations by Tanya Stesen of Dezigns by T

Library of Congress Cataloging-in-Publication Data

Nolan, Jameel D.
    The Ultimate Guide to Soy Candlemaking From Hobby Enthusiasts to Business Professionals / Jameel D. Nolan.
    ISBN: 978-0-578-03298-6

Visit us online at www.ultimateguidetosoycandlemaking.com

Contents

Foreword

I want to first thank God for allowing me the strength to write this book. The beginning process became a huge struggle for me. I started writing in November 2006, finishing only five pages. It wasn't until I attended church on November 4, 2007 that I was able to continue. My fiancé at the time encouraged me to go to the service and I'm so glad I went on that day. The pastor preached about overcoming our fears, procrastination, stagnation and simply being paralyzed by the unknown. He was *so* speaking directly to me. I had been in fear of the unknown for several years; scared to take the steps to write this book, scared to call on prospects to increase business sales and scared to write newsletters to spread awareness of my business. I had become paralyzed by my own fears. The pastor went on to say if we would just take the first step, God would part the rest of the way. Later on in the evening, that inner voice we all have spoke to me and said, "Go write the book and don't think about anything else." For once in my life I listened to that inner voice. In the next two hours I spent typing, I wrote seven additional pages and I just couldn't stop writing.

So I would like to thank Pastor Bert Neal of St. James United Methodist Church for delivering such a powerful message. I can always count on receiving my spiritual vitamin every time I step foot in there.

I would like to thank Burgundy James of Burgundy Soap Company for planting the seed in my brain to write this book about making soy candles and also for helping me to live a more environmentally friendly lifestyle. You have always been a strong supporter.

I would like to thank my parents Vanessa & Sam for always believing in my talents even when I didn't. Thank you for your financial support and advice over the years. You both have been there for me through it all and I thank you so much for loving me unconditionally.

I would like to thank my sister Monique for always trying to keep your baby sister in line and on track. You are an inspiration to me in so many ways and I love you very much!

I thank my handsome son Jarren for encouraging me to keep keeping on. Without you I am nothing but with you I can conquer the world. You have been with Mommy even before you knew about the candle business and now at seven years old you have helped to sell my products. You are my precious gem I will always cherish and truly a blessing.

Now, I would like to thank you, the reader (my candle making buddies), because if it wasn't for seeing all of your frustrating threads on the hundreds of forums I belong to, reading the challenges you have endured in making soy candles and seeing the misguided information given it wouldn't have motivated me to even write this book. So thank you for believing in my knowledge to provide you with accurate information so you, too, can have a successful home-based business.

Chapter 1: About the Author

In 1998, I got involved in making candles because I was tired of purchasing candles from stores that didn't have a good scent throw or didn't have much character. Having been blessed with an artistic talent, I knew I could make my own candles and have my candles look and smell better than what I was wasting my money on. At the time, I wasn't completely committed to candle making so, as with anything, it started off as a hobby. I can recall purchasing my first five pounds of paraffin wax…uggh (I will explain later). I had no knowledge of how to make candles so I did what anyone would do—researched the Internet on "how to make candles." To my surprise, there was a ton of information so I began my journey in perusing through the sites and found a few suppliers.

Approximately two weeks into researching, I figured it was time to start making candles. I started ordering supplies: paraffin wax, pouring pots, fragrances, dyes and wicks. I made two candles using paraffin wax and when these turned out nice I began to make more and more. Before I knew it, I had developed a love for candle making. But paraffin wax was definitely not my friend. After my first candle-making session I had wax drippings all over my kitchen floor. It seemed to have taken hours, if not days, to scrape all of the wax off my floor and counters. After doing this for about a year or two, I just couldn't make anymore paraffin candles and I wanted to find a better wax. To my surprise I came across gel wax. There was definitely an angel watching over me. I spent the next three weeks researching gel wax, the benefits and what materials were needed to get started on my next journey in candle making. I quickly fell in love with gel wax because it allowed my creativity to roam free.

I spent the next five years making gel candles while working full-time as a Sr. Administrative Assistant. I was eighteen years old when I started making them, and here I am ten years later, spreading my knowledge to you. In August of 2000, I realized that I was ready to take my hobby to the next level to make extra money but wasn't sure how to go about marketing my products. My first big event came when my sister was getting married and I made gel candle favors that coordinated with her color scheme, gold and white (clear). I made seventy-five gel candles in gold and seventy –five in clear, with each made in fluted jars. My mom and I wrapped the candles in gold and white tulle and attached my sister's personalized ribbon and, boom, we had gorgeous wedding favors. Everyone who attended the wedding loved my candles and many still have those favors to this very day, including my mom. After hearing everyone raving and fighting over the favors, I knew I was on to something.

I began to do well with gel candles and made a lot more money than what I was making hourly at my full-time job. My future in the candle making industry began to change after I had my son in 2002. Although making gel candles was fun and exciting, it also had a down side. Many of my customers began to complain about the odor once they blew the candle out. Gel wax is comprised of mineral oil (petroleum based) and resin, and is the hottest wax on the market. Trust me, I know. I can't tell you how many times I burnt myself. Many of my customers opted not to burn my candles because they were too pretty, so the candles would just sit. Well, after extensive research I found that if a gel candle sat too long it could cause the fragrance to pocket within the gel wax and could cause problems if burned. That really concerned me because I didn't want anything to happen to any of my customers by burning my candles. So back to the drawing board I went. In 2004, I met a wonderful new friend at my job (yes, I worked a full-time job and had a home-based business) who had her own home-based business manufacturing all natural bath and body products. If you're interested in learning how to make all natural soap the simple way, then click here:

http://www.simplesoapmaking.com/swres/kicompany.html

We immediately hit it off and began discussing business. She was interested in offering candles to compliment her bath and body line but she was only interested in natural candles. During this time I started hearing a little bit about soy candles and how these were far better than any other on the market. Of course, I had to do my research and I was amazed at the results. Soy wax candles seemed to be the best candles on the market. They burn clean, longer and virtually soot free compared to the traditional paraffin candles. I was in candle heaven once more!

I began to order supplies and began my testing with various wicks, fragrances and glass jars. Although soy candles were listed as the best candles on the market, the wax proved to be the most challenging to handle. Soy wax was known to have problems such as wet spots and crystallize specks. I experienced difficulty in getting a good scent throw from my existing fragrances. The last thing I wanted to do was invest in buying new fragrances when I already had over 150 different fragrances. After my many months of testing, my frustration grew and I was at my wits end with soy. I had signed new wholesale accounts and lost them just as fast because I had not achieved a high enough level to call myself a soy candle expert.

Well, I spent the next two years making soy candles with constant testing and researching, and I began to perfect my craft. After my trials and tribulations, including over ten thousand dollars spent in the first year in researching, I can honestly say it was worth it. My candle company was producing high volume soy candles using premium fragrance oils and lead-free wicks with our unique twist. I have found my niche in this industry and it has been working.

This eBook is not to bash any company's products but only to share what worked for my business. I tried several soy waxes, fragrance oils, wicks, and such from different companies and in this eBook you will find out what has worked for me and what has not. In my first two years of researching soy candles, going through the trials and tribulations, I spent approximately $17,000. Keep in mind, I was only making about $45,000 a year, had an infant son and other bills to take care of. Thinking back, I definitely would have done things differently. I don't want to see you go through what I went through. There's no need.

I decided to write an eBook to help those struggling or looking to perfect their soy candles. I want to save someone else time and money and help them avoid the costly mistakes I made. Right now, we have to hold on to our money and think smart to be successful in this business or any other type of business. I have found there were a lot of message boards out there where you can get a lot of good information from folks, but they will only tell you but so much. There's enough money out there for everyone and I'm here to help you get your cut. In the last ten years I have experienced a lot of ups and downs personally and financially; making candles was a definitely a way to turn my frustrations and disappointments in my life into a beautiful piece of art—an all natural soy candle. You will find happiness in what you do, joy when someone else raves of your candles and success when you go from a hobby enthusiast to a business professional.

For those seeking consulting, I offer business consulting and testing for a nominal fee through phone and via e-mail: info@ultimateguidetosoycandlemaking.com and I will respond to every email personally.

Thank you,

Jameel D. Nolan

Chapter 2: What is Soy Wax?

Soybean wax, often referred to simply as "soy wax," is produced with hydrogenated soybean oil. In 1993, inventor Michael Richards discovered it as he was looking for a cheaper alternative to beeswax. It was the first innovation in the candle industry for over a hundred years. Soy wax is a vegetable wax made from the oil of soybeans. After harvesting, the beans are cleaned, cracked, de-hulled, and rolled into flakes. The oil is then extracted from the flakes and hydrogenated. The hydrogenation process converts some of the fatty acids in the oil from unsaturated to saturated. This process dramatically alters the melting point of the oil, making it solid at room temperature. The leftover bean husks are commonly used as animal feed. The U.S. grows the vast majority of the world's soybeans, primarily in Illinois, Iowa, and Indiana.

The wax's main disadvantage is a lower melting point, resulting in candles which deform easily in hot weather and drip readily when burning.

What are the benefits?

Soy's greatest advantage is that it is completely renewable. Though the global reserves of oil are shrinking and paraffin prices are increasing, the only limit to the soy supply is how much we choose to grow.

In addition to sustainability, a well-made soy candle will burn cleanly and slowly, much to the delight of your customers. While the performance and beauty of these candles speak for themselves, soy wax is truly a marketer's dream. If you are making soy candles, you can market them as eco-friendly, renewable, American grown, sustainable, carbon neutral, and the list goes on and on.

The soybean is one of the most versatile products used today. It has been a high protein source for millions of people for thousands of years. It is found in many household products, crayons and other non-toxic products. If soy wax replaced paraffin wax, an estimated sixty million pounds of soybeans would be required for annual candle production.

Soy wax has the following features:

- Made with pure, 100% natural soybeans
- Burns longer, cooler and cleaner without soot buildup
- Easy to clean up with soap and hot water, eliminating solvents
- Very stable, allowing for long shelf life
- Made in the U.S. with domestically-grown crops
- Produced containing *no* Genetically Modified Material
- Manufactured meeting FDA and Kosher standards
- Renewable, sustainable resources requiring plant growth
- Biodegradable and free from pesticides and herbicides
- Not subject to animal testing

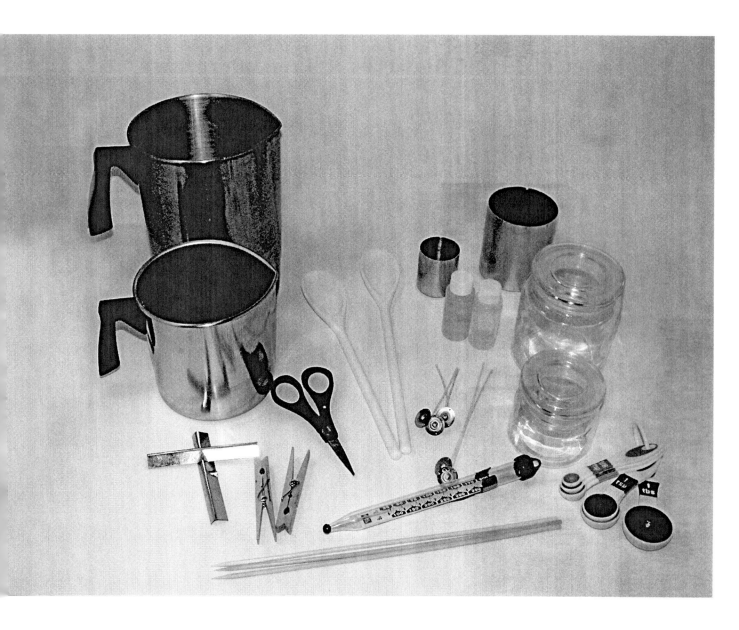

sic Tools for Candle Making

. 1lb Melting Pitcher
. 4lb Melting Pitcher
. Metal Wick Bars
. Wooden Clips
. Wicks
. Aluminum Mold

7. Wooden Skewers
8. Scents
9. Thermometer
10. Measuring Spoons
11. Glass Containers
12. Sharp Scissors

13. Votive Mold

Chapter 3: Tools, Materials & Basic Information

Supplies Needed:

Dual Electric Hot Plate (Wal-Mart)
EcoSoya™ CB 135
EcoSoya™ Pillar Blend
Golden Brands 464
Fractionated Coconut Oil
Wick Bars or Clothesline Clips
Dye Chips (Optional)
Hair Dryer or Professional Heat Gun
Fragrance Oils
Wicks
Warning Labels
Containers - Glass or Travel Tin
1 lb & 4 lb Aluminum Melting Pitchers
Clean Empty Food Cans
Timer
Digital Scale
Thermometer
Potholder Glove
Plastic Ice Trays
Wooden Skewers
Polyurethane Plastic Spoons
Grey or White Putty

Dual Electric Hot Plate

We have always used a dual hot plate instead of the double boiler many other companies

suggest. You have the option to use which ever one is convenient to you. In this eBook

we will discuss using an electric hot plate because that worked better for us.

EcoSoya™ CB 135

EcoSoya™ CB 135 has excellent adhesion to containers without preheating, requires

only one pour, has an excellent scent throw with both fragrances and essential oils, and a

creamy white appearance with some potential to bloom (white frosting) when using dyes.

EcoSoya™ Pure Soy

EcoSoya™ CB Pure Soy has excellent adhesion to containers without preheating, requires only one pour, has an excellent scent throw with both fragrances and essential oils, and a creamy white appearance with good resistance to bloom (white frosting) formation when using dyes.

Golden Brand 464

This soy-based additive enables the soy to be poured at a hotter temperature, reducing frosting and increasing fragrance oil (FO) load. This wax is able to hold a lot of fragrance oils but has a much lower melt point. The lower melt point makes these candles difficult to ship during the summer months.

Where can you find the tools and materials?

Tools	Supplier / Store	Website (if applicable)
Dual or Single Hot Plate	Wal-Mart or Target	
Professional Wax Melter	Candle Science	www.candlescience.com
Clothespins	Dollar Store or Wal-Mart	
Timer	Wal-Mart or Target	
Thermometer	Wal-Mart or Michael's	
Plastic Ice Trays	Wal-Mart	
Polyurethane Plastic Spoons	Dollar Store or Wal-Mart	
Pot Holder Glove	Dollar Store	
Digital Scales	eBay or Bitter Creek	www.candlesupply.com
Wooden Skewers	Dollar Store or Wal-Mart	
Professional Heat Gun	Home Depot or Lowe's	www.michaels.com
Candle Supplies	**Supplier**	**Website**
EcoSoya™ CB 135 Soy Wax	Candle Science	www.candlescience.com
EcoSoya™ Pillar Blend Soy Wax	Candle Science	www.candlescience.com
Golden Brands 464 Soy Wax	Candle Science	www.candlescience.com
Fractionated Coconut Oil	Rainbow Meadow	www.rainbowmeadow.com
Wick Bars	Candle Science	www.candlescience.com
Dye Chips, Dye Blocks, Liquid Dye	Candle Science	www.candlescience.com
Fragrance Oils	See Supplier Page	

Candle Supplies	Supplier	Website
Wicks	Candle Science	www.candlescience.com
Plain Labels	Online Labels or Brown Kraft Labels	www.onlinelabels.com www.brownkraftlabels.com
Glass Containers	See Resource Page	
Travel Tins	SKS Bottle or Specialty Bottle	www.sks-bottle.com www.specialtybottle.com
1 lb & 4 lb Melting Pitchers	Candle Science	www.candlescience.com

Measurements

Here is an easy-to-follow conversion chart:

1 pound	=	16 ounces
1 cup	=	8 fluid ounces / 16 tablespoons / 48 teaspoons
2 cups	=	1 pint
4 cups	=	1 quart
1 ounce	=	30 grams
1 fluid ounce	=	2 tablespoons
1 tablespoon	=	½ fluid ounce
1 tablespoon	=	3 teaspoons
½ ounce fragrance to 1 pound of wax	=	3% fragrance
1 ounce fragrance to 1 pound of wax	=	6% fragrance
1 ½ ounce fragrance to 1 pound of wax	=	9% fragrance

Color Blending

Green	+	Blue	=	**Teal**
Blue	+	Red	=	**Purple**
Yellow	+	Blue	=	**Green**
Red	+	Yellow	=	**Orange**
White	+	Red	=	**Pink**
White	+	Blue	=	**Lt. Blue**

Soy Candle Burn Times:

Candle Type	Burn Time
2 oz.	15-20 hours
4 oz.	25-30 hours
5 oz.	40-45 hours
8 oz.	60 hours
10 oz.	75 hours
12 oz.	80 hours
16 oz.	100-125 hours
26 oz. & 27 oz.	180-200 hours
Tea Lights	10-12 hours

Candle Type	Burn Time
2 oz. Votives	20 hours
3 oz. Votives	30 hours
3 x 3 Pillar	60-80 hours
4 x 4 Pillar	120-140 hours

Conducting a Proper Burn Test

Once you have successfully made your candles and it's been at least forty-eight hours then it's time to test burn your creation. Follow the below steps to ensure your candle is safe to market:

1. If I am testing multiple candles, I always label mine by using a 2 x 4 label. I suggest you do one of two things:

    a. Include all pertinent information on label such as: wicks used, wax used, amount of additives, amount of dye (if applicable), pouring temp, etc.

    b. Or you can put all of this information on your candle test sheet and have each sheet labeled 1, 2, 3, etc. Place a label on the actual candle indicating the matching test number from your candle test sheet

2. Trim the wick(s) to ¼ inch.

3. Begin by lighting your candles and recording the time. It is very critical to keep an eye on your candles while they are burning, as well as watching the time. I recommend having a timer and setting it for thirty minutes. You should check your candles every thirty minutes and record the results. When I test my candles I place all candles being tested in a line up in my kitchen. I first write down the pertinent information prior to lighting.

4. After approximately two hours your candle should have reached a full melt pool. Make sure you record the results. Was there mushrooming, soot, scent throw, etc?

5. After four hours of burning, the candle should have achieved the desired diameter and your candle should have ½ inch of melted wax. If the wick mushroomed, there was soot, or your candle had more than ½ inch of melted wax, then there's a possibility the wick was too large.

6. Allow candle to cool down and re-solidify. Repeat steps 3, 4, and 5 until the candle has completely burned.

I also highly recommend having your friends and family members to test your candles. Everyone has a different sense of smell. One fragrance could be too strong to one person but too light to another. I have found at times it was difficult for me to smell my candles because I was constantly inhaling the fragrances. So definitely get friends, neighbors or family members involved during your test-burning sessions.

Curing

It takes up to five to seven days for soy candles to cure using fragrance oils and up to two to three weeks using essential oils. Don't be discouraged by this. In my experience, when you are using quality fragrance oils you can typically burn your candles to test scent throw within forty-eight to seventy-two hours. Curing allows the soy candle to harden over time and achieve maximum scent throw.

I typically fill candle orders at the time of ordering, ensuring my customers receive fresh soy candles. I always include a card explaining the proper maintenance in burning them.

Your card can read, For best results it is best to wait five days before burning your soy candle to ensure you receive the strongest scent throw possible. Your customers will not have a problem with this at all. It's better to notify your customers upfront rather than receiving disgusted e-mails later.

Candle Texture

There have been concerns of the candle texture after a soy candle has burned. The texture can vary, and includes things like cracking at the top and frost. You should not worry about this at all. The candle is likely to change its appearance based on many factors, such as the temperature in the room, drafts, and the amount of fragrance or essential oils used. I personally would not waste my energy on how the candle looks after burning but rather focus your energy on how well the candle is burning.

Melt Pool

What is melt pool?

Melt pool is the amount of liquid wax burning per hour and per inch in diameter of the container. Your goal is to get your soy candle to burn completely to the jar and then straight down. As weird as it may sound, soy wax has a memory. On the very first burn, it is important for the soy candle to burn completely to the container so that on each and every burn thereafter you will receive a full melt pool and very little waxy residue remaining. If the candle does not burn completely to the container the very first time this will cause a tunneling effect, therefore wasting a lot of soy wax which won't be burned It is very important to express this on any literature you provide to your customers.

When your candle has achieved full melt pool with very little to no mushrooming and as well as a wonderful scent throw…you have achieved your ultimate goal! A soy candle that smells great and leaves very little soy wax residue is considered a well-made candle.

Chapter 4: Making Soy Container Candles

PROJECT #1 – 5 oz. Apothecary Soy Candles – DYE FREE

Materials Needed: EcoSoya™ CB 135 or GB 464 Soy Wax
Thermometer
Fractionated Coconut Oil
5 oz. Apothecary Jar
Eco Wick 6 or 8
Wick Bar or Clothesline Clips
1 to 1.5 oz. Fragrance Oil
Plastic Spoon
Timer

In my experience in working with soy wax, I find it's best to have the room in which you're making candles to be around 72°F Typically, my candle room is like a sauna, because I usually keep my room around seventy-five to seventy-eight degrees, but that's what works for me. The temperature can be what's comfortable for you but definitely not too cold.

Let's get started!

Always set your timer for fifteen to twenty minutes when you are melting wax. You don't want to forget your wax is melting. I have done that several times.

Step 1: Wipe out any dust or cardboard residue you may see in your containers with either a towel or my personal preference, paper towels. Add your wick. When adding your wick I recommend using Glue Dots™, or a less expensive way is using a glue gun with high temperature glue sticks. Glue sticks can be found at Michael's or Wal-Mart for under two dollars. I personally prefer Glue Dots™ simply because it takes less time when wicking jars and these secure far better to the jar than hot glue does.

Step 2: Scoop out soy wax using a measuring cup and pour into the aluminum pot. You do not have to worry about measuring the wax until it has completely melted. Set your electric hot plate on medium and allow wax to melt to 185°F. While your wax is melting, this would be a good time to heat your containers. I usually use a heater to warm up my jars, but others use a heat gun or blow dryer and some people don't heat their jars at all. I recommend heating because then the wax adheres to the glass container leaving no to very little wet spots.

When you become an expert at making candles you will begin to develop your own routine and times for heating your jars. From my personal experience, I keep my jars in the oven until I'm ready to pour my wax. The reason why you should heat your jars prior to pouring your wax is because it will allow the jar and wax to cool at the same temperature and this also eliminates wet spots and enables good glass adhesion

Step 3: Once your wax has melted, use your thermometer to check the temperature. When your temperature has reached 185°F, remove it from the heat source. Place an empty pouring pot on your digital scale and pour 1 lb. (16 oz.) of wax. Add a teaspoon of fractionated coconut oil per pound of wax, as this will help to strengthen your fragrance oil. Add your fragrance oil by weighing it at 1 oz. to 1.5 oz. Stir well for at least two minutes. (Be sure you do not allow the wax to be on heat after the scent has been added since this will cause the fragrance to evaporate.) I use aluminum votive molds with the fragrance labeled on each mold. Make sure the fragrances you are using are specifically for candle making. *Never use alcohol-based fragrance oils.*

Note: 1 oz. of fragrance oil will scent 1 lb. of wax. There are times when you may have to add ½ oz. more fragrance oil, but after testing several times you will become experienced as to which fragrances require a larger amount. But if you order your fragrances from the companies listed in the resource section of this book, then only 1 oz. will suffice. You will find that some fragrances don't give a strong scent throw at all, so know that it's just the nature of the fragrance oils and essential oils and not a problem with your methods or with the soy wax. Testing fragrances can definitely be trial and error, not to mention expensive. When making the candles, stir the fragrance well to blend and bind into the wax. Allow soy wax to cool to around 125°F. If your candle does not have a good scent throw after three days of curing, then get rid of that fragrance.

Step 4: Now that your wax has cooled down to 125°F, it's time to pour. Slowly pour the wax into the container, straighten the wick and secure it with a wick bar or clothesline clips. Clothesline clips are very inexpensive and highly recommended for making candles. These can be found at Wal-Mart for about three dollars for one hundred or more.

Step 5: For best results, allow candle to cool at room temperature for twenty-four hours. Soy candles will need to cure for at least a week prior to selling. This allows the fragrance to strengthen and aids in achieving a good scent throw.

Step 6: Trim wick to ¼ inch before lighting. Remember to do this each time you light your candle. Wipe your candle jar using Windex® to remove any waxy residue or greasy handprints.

CONGRATULATIONS!! Your first candle is complete. ENJOY.

It does take some practice to get your candle right but if you use the proper methods and have lots of patience, you will get it. The steps that have been provided above are the steps that I used in my candle business. I have wasted a lot of money trying different wicks, dye powders, dye chips, liquid dye and everything else just trying to make the best soy candle. I want to help others to eliminate wasting money like I did.

PROJECT #2 –16 oz. Apothecary Soy Candles – ADD DYE CHIPS

Materials Needed: EcoSoya™ CB 135 or GB 464 Soy Wax
Thermometer
Fractionated Coconut Oil
Dye Chips
Fragrance Oils
16 oz. Apothecary Container Jars
Eco 4 – Double Wick
Wick Bars or Clothesline clips
Aluminum Melting Pitcher
Plastic Spoon

Start by heating your oven to 200°F. At this point, all of your containers should be clean. Place your clean jars into the oven for five to ten minutes. Remember to use your potholder when removing glass containers from any hot surface. **Follow Steps 1 and 2 from Project #1.**

Step 3: Once your wax has melted, place another aluminum pouring pot on your digital scale and pour 1 lb. (16 oz.) of wax into the pot. Add dye chip and stir well. If you see little particles at the bottom then simply place the melting pitcher back on heat until dye particles completely dissolve. Remove wax from heat. After the temperature has cooled to 165°F, add a teaspoon of fractionated coconut oil per pound of wax, as this will strengthen your fragrance oil. Weigh your fragrance oil to 1 oz. and add it to the wax. (Be sure you do not allow the wax to be on heat after the scent has been added since this will cause the fragrance to evaporate.) Stir well.

Follow Steps: 4, 5, 6 and 7 from Project #1

Note: When you're first starting out, I recommend not adding dye until you have completely tested your candles. Use as many or as little dye chips you desire to achieve your choice of color. Add more chips for darker colored candles. You do not have to weigh dye.

CONGRATULATIONS!! You have now made your first candle using dye.

Advanced Soy Candles – Creating Layers

PROJECT #3 –16 oz. Apothecary Soy Candles–ADD DYE CHIPS

Materials Needed: EcoSoya™ CB135 or GB 464 Soy Wax
Thermometer
Fractionated Coconut Oil
Dye Chips
Fragrance Oils
16 oz. Apothecary Container Jars
Eco 6 –Double Wick
Wick Bars or Clothesline clips
Aluminum Melting Pitcher
Aluminum Can
Plastic Spoon

Follow Steps 1 and 2 from Project #1 above.

Step 3: Once your wax has melted, place another aluminum pouring pot on your digital scale and pour 1 lb. (16 oz.) of wax into it. Add a teaspoon of fractionated coconut oil per pound of wax as this will strengthen your fragrance oil. Weigh your fragrance oil to 1 oz. and add it to the wax. Stir well. Then pour some wax into another melting pitcher, or clean the unused can, and add the desired colored dye chip(s) and stir well. If you see little particles at the bottom then simply place the melting pitcher back on heat until dye particles completely dissolve. Stir well. (Be sure you do not allow any scented wax to be on heat after the scent has been added since this will cause the fragrance to evaporate. If you have to do this, simply add more approximately ½ ounce of fragrance.)

Step 4: Now that your wax has cooled down to 125°F, it's time to pour. Slowly pour your first layer of wax into the container, straighten the wick, and secure it with a wick bar or clothesline clips. Allow the first layer of wax to cool completely (four to five hours) before adding the next layer. I recommend heating the area of the jar with a heat gun or blow dryer where you will be pouring your second layer of wax to ensure good glass adhesion.

Step 5: Once you have poured all layers of wax, allow candle to cool at room temperature for twenty-four hours.

Step 6: Trim wick to ¼ inch before lighting. Remember to do this each time you light your candle.

CONGRATULATIONS!! Your first layered candle is complete. ENJOY.

Materials Needed: EcoSoya™ CB135 or GB 464 Soy Wax (Container Blend)
EcoSoya™ Pillar Blend
Thermometer
Dye Chips
Fractionated Coconut Oil
Fragrance Oils
Shallow Baking Pan
Sharp Knife
16 oz. Apothecary Container Jars
Eco 6 –Double Wick
Wick Bars or Clothesline clips
Aluminum Melting Pitcher
Aluminum Cans (3)
Plastic Spoon

Making Wax Chips

1. Melt approximately 9 oz. of EcoSoya™ Pillar Blend soy wax to 185°F.

2. Once soy wax has completely melted, allow the wax to cool to around 175°F and add ¼ teaspoon of fragrance oil and stir well. Then pour 3 oz. of the scented pillar soy wax in the aluminum cans (from your canned foods). Add your choice of colored dye chips to each of the cans and stir well. Keep in mind you are using a small portion of wax so a full dye chip will not be necessary. Simply shave off part of the dye chip to achieve your desired color results.

3. Allow wax to cool around 155°F and then pour into the shallow baking pan. The wax should cool completely, leaving no liquid wax.

4. Once wax has completely hardened but is still slightly soft to the touch, begin to cut small squares using a sharp knife. Allow the squares to cool completely until they harden. Repeat this process for additional colored chunks.

Making the Candle

1. Warm your container slightly and then double wick using Eco 6. The wicks should be spaced about an inch apart.

2. Begin filling your container with the different color wax chunks. Gently shake it to settle them. Make sure to keep the wicks centered.

3. Melt approximately 16 oz. of EcoSoya™ or Golden Brands soy wax to 185°F.

4. Once soy wax has completely melted, allow the wax to cool to around 175°F, and then add a teaspoon of fractionated coconut oil per pound of wax as this will strengthen your fragrance oil. Add 1 oz. of fragrance oil and stir well.

5. Allow soy wax to cool to around 150°F, then slowly pour your wax into the container and tap gently to release any air bubbles. You may need to do a re-pour as the wax settles and cools.

6. Remember to keep the temperature in the room as warm as possible to achieve good glass adhesion with minimal wet spots and frosting. I kept an electric heater in my candle room, making the temperature around 76°F.

PROJECT #5 – Swirl Soy Candles

Materials Needed: EcoSoya™ CB 135 or GB 464 Soy Wax (Container Blend)
Thermometer
Dye Chips
Fractionated Coconut Oil
Fragrance Oils
8 oz. Travel Tin Container
Eco 10
Wick Bars or Clothesline Clips
Aluminum Melting Pitcher
Aluminum Can
Toothpick or Wooden Skewer
Plastic Spoon

1. Follow the steps above to make a container candle.

2. Pour about an ounce of melted wax into aluminum or stainless steel can. Add a teaspoon of fractionated coconut oil per pound of wax as this will strengthen your fragrance oil. Add dye and stir well.

3. Take your remaining scented, dye-free wax and pour into the 8 oz. travel tin—do not fill completely.

4. Slowly pour a little of your colored wax into your tin. Using a toothpick or wooden skewer, gently create swirls.

Swirl soy candles will look nice with a single color, or you can get really creative and use multiple colors.

Chapter 5: Making Soy Pillar Candles

PROJECT #1–3 x 3 Round Pillar Soy Candle–DYE FREE

Materials Needed: EcoSoya™ Pillar Blend
Thermometer
3 x 3 Aluminum Round Mold - **Note: Make sure your pillar molds have pre-drilled holes prior to purchasing**
Mold Release
Eco Wick 12
Wick Bar or Clothesline Clips
1 to 1.5 oz. Fragrance Oil
Polyurethane Plastic Spoon
Timer

There are many different shapes and sizes of pillar molds. The molds are manufactured out of sheet metal, aluminum, polyurethane plastic, and silicone. Molds made out of aluminum and sheet metals are very durable and will last for many years.

Step 1: Begin scooping out your EcoSoya™ Pillar Blend wax into the melting pitcher. Allow wax to melt to 185°F. While your wax is melting, lay out an old newspaper to catch any spills and then lay out the pillar mold(s).

Step 2: Thread your Eco 12 wick into the wick hole of the mold. The wick hole is at the base of the mold. If you are experiencing difficulty threading the wick through the wick hole, simply dip the wick into some melted wax and roll it with your fingers to make a pointed end. Secure the end with a wick screw and then take a little wad of either the grey or white putty and place it over the top of the wick screw. The putty will help to avoid wax leakage. Make sure the wick screw is secure but not super tight as this can cause damage to the wick or mold. This area will turn out to be the top of your finished candle.

Step 3: While keeping the wick as straight as possible, secure with a wick pin or tie it to a wooden skewer.

Step 4: Once your wax has completely melted, add fragrance oil and stir well. I recommend adding your fragrance oil first before adding your dye(s) so you can see that each has mixed well into the wax.

Step 5: Allow wax to cool to around 140-145°F. While your pillar wax is cooling, spray a thin layer of mold release inside your mold(s). A silicone spray or PAM cooking spray is suitable. This helps to aid in the release of the finished pillar candle. Mold release spray is especially recommended for new molds.

Step 6: With the pillar wax now at the proper pouring temperature (140-145°F), fill your pillar mold(s) to ½ inch from top of mold. Save some wax to do a re-pour. Do not return the melting pitcher to heat.

Step 7: Allow your wax to cool. Once the wax has solidified but is a rather warm, poke relief hole using wooden skewers in the base of the candle to accommodate for shrinkage. Position the relief holes around the wick, about an inch in depth. Several relief holes may be required throughout the process. Allow the candle to cool completely, which could take several hours and for larger pillars it could take up to twenty-four hours.

Step 8: Take your leftover soy wax from Step 6 and re-melt it. Make sure the temperature is five to ten degrees hotter than before. The re-melt should be hotter because it aids in adhesion between layers. Once your wax is at the appropriate temperature, fill the sinkholes of your candle. Again, do not fill to the top of the mold. Simply fill just above the first level to avoid horizontal seam lines.

Step 9: Allow your pillar candle to completely cool. Now, remove the putty (mold sealer) and the wick screw. Your candle should slide right out of the mold. If you experience difficulty with it coming out, place it in the freezer for five minutes or in the refrigerator for fifteen minutes. This will cause the wax to shrink and separate from the mold.

Where the wick is attached to the wick bar or wooden skewer is the bottom of the candle. Trim the wick on this end, using a pair of sharp scissors. The wick should be trimmed flush with the base of the candle.

PROJECT #2–3 x 3 Round Pillar Soy Candle–ADD DYE CHIPS

Materials Needed: EcoSoya™ Pillar Blend
Thermometer
3 x 3 Aluminum Round Mold
Dye Chips (any color)
Mold Release
Eco Wick 12
Wick Bar or Clothesline Clips
1 to 1.5 oz. Fragrance Oil
Polyurethane Plastic Spoon
Timer

Begin by following **Steps 1, 2, and 3** from Project #1.

Step 4: Once your wax has completely melted at the appropriate temperature of 185°F, add your fragrance oil and stir well for two minutes. By adding your fragrance oil first, you will be able to see that it has thoroughly mixed into the wax. Then add your dye chip(s) in any color you desire. Stir well.

Then simply follow **Steps 5, 6, 7, 8 and 9** from Project #1.

Chapter 6: Making Soy Votives, Tart Candles & Aroma Melts

PROJECT #1–Soy Votive Candles

Materials Needed: EcoSoya™ Pillar Blend
Thermometer
Fractionated Coconut Oil
Any type of Aluminum Votive Mold
Mold Release
Eco Wick 4 or 6
Wick Bar or Clothesline Clips
1 to 1.5 oz. Fragrance Oil
Dye (Optional)
Polyurethane Plastic Spoon
Timer

Votives are one of the easiest molded candles to make. A typical votive will burn for approximately ten to fifteen hours and will generally consume all of the wax if it is properly placed in a snug-fit votive holder. Votive candles are not intended to be free-standing candles.

Many chandlers choose to use wick pins for their votives because they feel it's easier or faster. I think differently. I think adding the wick pins makes it a two-step process, which is more time and work. Also, each time I have used the pins, my votives ended up cracking in half, not to mention the wicks don't seem to be secure.

Step 1: Begin by scooping out your EcoSoya™ Pillar Blend wax into the melting pitcher. Allow wax to melt to 185°F. While your wax is melting, lay out an old newspaper to catch any spills and then lay out the votive molds, leaving space between each one.

Step 2: Once your wax has completely melted, add fragrance oil and, if you want, dye chip(s) and stir well. I recommend adding your fragrance oil before the dye so you can see that each has mixed well into the wax. Then add your dye chip(s) by following Step 4 from Project #1 –3 x 3 Round Pillar Soy Candle.

Step 3: Allow wax to cool to around 140-145°F. While your pillar wax is cooling, it would be a good time to spray a thin layer of mold release inside your molds. A silicone spray or PAM cooking spray is suitable. This helps to aid in the release of the finished votive candle. Mold release spray is especially recommended for new molds.

Step 4: With the pillar wax now at the proper pouring temperature (140-145°F), fill your votive molds to the lip of the mold—filling any lower than this can cause seam lines in your finished candle votive. Save any wax just in case you have to do a re-pour.

Step 5: Allow your wax to cool. While the wax is cooling, begin to prepare your pre-tabbed Eco 4 wicks by straightening them. The wax will begin to congeal around the lip of the mold, which is an indication the wax is beginning to harden at the bottom. Insert your pre-tabbed wicks. The tab will automatically stick to the bottom. Gently straighten the wick and then you can use a wick tab or clothespin to hold it in place (not always needed).

FYI: Do not add the wick to the wax if it has not started to congeal. If the wax is too hot this will cause the wick to move and you risk it not being centered.

Allow your votive candle to completely cool for about four hours to see if any shrinkage or sinkholes occur. Reheat your leftover wax to about 180°F (hotter than initial pour). This increase in temperature ensures adhesion between the layers.

Now votive candles should completely cool down for at least twenty-four hours.

Step 6: It's time to remove your votive candles from the mold. They should simply slide right out of mold but if you're experiencing some difficulty, try placing them in the freezer for a few minutes. Remove them from the freezer and the votives should come right out. If you still experience problems, then place them back in the freezer for five minutes.

Voila! You have made your first votive candles. ENJOY.

PROJECT #2–Soy Tart Candles

Materials Needed: EcoSoya™ Pillar Blend
Thermometer
Fractionated Coconut Oil
Any type of Aluminum Tart Mold
TL 28 or TL 31
1 oz. Fragrance Oil (for each 1 lb. of wax)
Dye (Optional)
Polyurethane Plastic Spoon
Timer

Follow the same steps as above in making votive candles. Simply change from a votive mold to a tart mold. Tarts can either be candles or aroma melts that can be added to a candle warmer.

If you decide to make a tart candle, simply add TL 28 or TL 31 wicks, which can be found at www.candlescience.com.

Tart candles are perfect for wedding, baby shower or party favors. A great way to wrap the tarts as favors would be to use a complimenting color of tulle and ribbon. Doing this will drastically change the look of your tart candle. These are also great to give out as samplers.

Always keep in mind that presentation is everything. Making a great soy candle isn't enough—how you present that great candle will close the sale.

PROJECT #3–Soy Aroma Melts

Materials Needed: EcoSoya™ Pillar Blend
Thermometer
Plastic Ice Trays
Fractionated Coconut Oil
1 to 1.5 oz. Fragrance Oil
Dye (Optional)
Polyurethane Plastic Spoon
Timer

BEST SELLERS!! The aroma melts that I sell are one of my best sellers. I started out by simply giving these out as samplers, as a way to advertise my business. Well, I have since started packaging these and they're so easy and inexpensive to make. These will last for up to three to six weeks.

One of my wholesale customers buys these individually from me and resells just one aroma melt for one dollar.

I purchase ice trays from Wal-Mart, at $0.97 for a four-pack that will hold fourteen melts each. When I last checked, it cost me around $0.18 to make. I purchase 3 x 4 ziplock bags from Michael's for $1.49 for a pack of 100. Wal-Mart also sells these bags.

Step 1: Begin scooping out your EcoSoya™ Pillar Blend wax into the melting pitcher. Allow wax to melt to 185°F. While your wax is melting, lay out an old newspaper to catch any spills and then lay out the four ice trays, leaving space between each one.

Step 2: Once your wax has completely melted, measure out 1 lb. of wax and then add 1 tp. of coconut oil, 1 oz. of fragrance oil and, if you want, dye chip(s) and stir well. I recommend adding your coconut and fragrance oil first so you can see that each has mixed well into the wax. Then add your dye chip(s). I always add extra fragrance oil to my aroma melts because the customer is not burning these—they're used to scent areas like the home or office.

Step 3: Allow wax to cool to around 140-145°F. After the wax has cooled, pour into ice trays and allow melts to cool for twenty-four hours. If you're crunched for time, then wait until the wax has started to congeal and then place the ice tray in the freezer to harden for about ten minutes. Then pop them out. If you experience some problems with the melts not releasing, then simply place them back in freezer for a couple of minutes.

Below is the information I recommend placing on your label so your customers, friends and family will know how to use the tarts:

Place a tart in a wax warmer and enjoy the
soothing aroma throughout your home.
For wax warmers only! To change fragrances, place
melting container in freezer for five minutes and
pop out the old fragrance melt.

You can definitely change the content to suit your needs.

Voila! **You have now made twenty-eight highly scented Soy Aroma Melts.**

These melts are probably one of the *best* and most *inexpensive* ways to promote your business. You will definitely have to explain to your potential customer that in order to get the full effects of the melt they will need to have either an oil burner or an electric warmer. Also, when your business grows this will be an excellent accessory to add to your candle line.

Advanced Soy Candles–Creating Layers

PROJECT #4–Votives, Tarts and Aroma Melts–ADD DYE CHIPS

Materials Needed: EcoSoya™ Pillar Blend
Thermometer
Dye Chips
Fragrance Oils
Aluminum Votive Mold, Tart Mold or Ice Tray
TL 28 or TL 31 (optional)
Aluminum Melting Pitcher
Aluminum Can
Thermometer
Plastic Spoon

Follow Steps 1 and 2 from Project #1 above.

Step 3: Once your wax has melted, place another aluminum pouring pot on your digital scale and pour 1 lb. (16 oz.) of wax into the pot. Add dye chip and stir well. If you see little particles at the bottom then simply place the melting pitcher back on heat until dye particles completely dissolve. Remove wax from heat. After the temperature has cooled to 165°F, add a teaspoon of fractionated coconut oil per pound of wax, as this will strengthen your fragrance oil. Weigh your fragrance oil to 1 oz. and add it to the wax. (Be sure you do not allow the wax to be on heat after the scent has been added since this will cause the fragrance to evaporate.) Stir well.

Step 4: Now that your wax has cooled down to 125°F, it's time to pour. Slowly pour your first layer of wax into the mold or ice tray, straighten the wick, and secure it with a wick bar or clothesline clips. Allow the first layer of wax to cool completely (forty-five minutes to one hour) before adding the next layer.

Step 5: Once you have poured all layers of wax, allow the candle to cool at room temperature for twenty-four hours.

Step 6: Trim wick to ¼ inch before lighting. Remember to do this each time you light your candle.

Voila! **Congratulations!! Your first layered votive, tart or aroma melt is complete. ENJOY.**

Chapter 7: Fragrance Guide

Scent Mixing

What will set you apart from any other candle company will be your fragrances. Creating your own unique, customized fragrances either by combining two or more fragrances to make one or working with a manufacturer in customizing oils for your business will set you apart from the other companies.

Below is a partial list of the type of fragrances you can mix together to come up with a unique creation. You can also change the name to set you apart from the other candle companies.

Add This	To This	And You Get
Cinnamon	Bayberry	Cinnaberry
Chocolate	Peppermint or Candy Cane	Mint Chocolate
Vanilla	Patchouli	Vanilla Patchouli
Strawberry	Kiwi	Strawberry Kiwi
Lime	Peppermint	Mojito Cocktail
Apple	Cinnamon	Apple Cinnamon
Rose	Vanilla	Baby Powder
Lavender	Chamomile	Lavender Chamomile
Rosemary	Peppermint	Rosemary Mint

Create the Right Mood

Fragrance has everything to do with creating the right mood. Some scents make women and men feel attractive or empowered. There are scientific studies that have linked scents to the emotional side of our brains. When I smell certain fragrances, I'm reminded of past childhood experiences, special times, and events.

Essential oils are beneficial in achieving the right mood. Below is a list of oils to consider when creating your line of soy candles:

Emotional Balance

The below list of essential oils aid in lessening emotional irritability, anger, grief, depression, insomnia and fatigue. They also encourage excitement, cheerfulness, and mental clarity, just to list a few of the benefits. Research the oil prior to making candles or blending to know what exact aromatherapy you are looking to achieve.

Frankincense (Boswellia carteri)

Lemon (Citrus limon)

Orange (Citrus aurantium var. amara)

Chamomile, Roman (Chamaemelum nobile)

Mandarin (Citrus reticulata)

Lavender (Lavandula angustifola)

Peppermint (Mentapiperita)

Patchouli (Pogostemon patchouli)

Pine (Pinus sylvestris)

Rosemary (Rosmarinus offcinalis)

Ginger (Zingiber officinale)

Clary Sage (Salvia sclarea)

Chapter 8: Selecting the Right Wick

What is the best wick to use? Choosing the right wick seems to be the debate among chandlers. Everyone has their own preference of what they consider to be the "right" wick. I have used all types of wicks and have spent a lot of money doing the research. So I'm here to tell you this is the end of researching a ton of wicks—save your money for more important stuff.

Testing wicks, I would say, is the most challenging part of candle making. This is usually where some people give up. But please don't be discouraged. I read thread after thread on various Internet forums and many people would discuss the wicks they were using and which soy wax. When reading some of the posts, I found it difficult to understand why several of us could use the same wick with the same soy wax but receive different results in terms of burning. Granted, you can receive different results when different variables are involved, such as additives, dyes, and the fragrance percentage. But in the beginning stages of making candles you should not be adding any dye or fragrance oil to your wax until you have decided on a choice for wicks. And this is where we ran into problems. There were a few of us who were using the same wick, same wax and no additives but we all received different results…how can this be? I came to the conclusion it was impossible and realized that some may have figured out what worked, but of course didn't want to share it because this would allow others to be on the same level. Some would consider it to be a company trade secret.

I have found the Eco series wicks to be the best when making soy candles. I have tried HTP, Hemp and Zinc series. I never recommend using wicks that have a metal core because you will *always* experience mushrooming and poor burning qualities.

Here are my wick recommendations:

GLASS CONTAINERS	WICK SIZE	BEST	2ND BEST
5 oz. Apothecary	Eco 6	Eco 6	Hemp 838
10 oz. Apothecary – 2 wick	Eco 4 or 6	Eco 6	
16 oz. Apothecary – 2 wick	Eco 4 or 6	Eco 6	Eco 4
26 oz. Apothecary – 2 wick	Eco 8	Eco 8	
4 oz. Morgan	Eco 4 or 6	Eco 4	Eco 6
12 oz. Morgan – 2 wick	Eco 6 or Eco 8	Eco 6	Eco 8
2 oz. Travel Tin	Eco 2	Eco 2	
4 oz. Travel Tin	Eco 4	Eco 4	
8 oz. Travel Tin	Eco 12 or 14	Eco 14	
8 oz. Madison	Eco 8 or 10	Eco 10	
5 oz. Bulb	Eco 6	Eco 6	
9 oz. Bulb	Eco 8	Eco 8	

PILLAR CANDLES	WICK SIZE	BEST	2ND BEST
3 x 3 Round Concave	Eco 12	Eco 12	
4 x 4 Square	Eco 14	Eco 14	
Crescent Moon	Eco 14	Eco 14	
VOTIVE, TART, TEALIGHT CANDLES	**WICK SIZE**	**BEST**	**2ND BEST**
Flared, Round and Octagon	Eco 4	Eco 4	
Square	Eco 4 or 6	Eco 6	Eco 4
Tart	TL 28 or TL 31	TL28	TL31
Tea Light	TL 28 or TL 31	TL28	TL31

Chapter 9: Creating Your Own Labels

There's no need to go out and immediately spend a lot of money having labels designed until you are in a position to sell your candles. It can get crazy having to make your own candles and print your labels. I recommend having a standard label with the scent name on it and a clip art or logo that best suits your company name or image you're trying to achieve.

I recommend having this important stuff somewhere on your label:

- Company Name

- Fragrance

- Container Size

- Company Web Site (if applicable)

The style you're going with, whether its primitive country, trendy or upscale, will determine what type of label material you decide on. Most primitive country is printed on Kraft labels, upscale would ideally be printed on clear labels, and trendy is typically printed on white or clear. But it's totally up to you. If you have decided to keep this as a hobby, simply include the fragrance name.

I set time aside each week to print out my labels and place them in a bin sorter. This helps when I'm short on time.

Brown Kraft Labels
3410 Cornelius Drive
Bloomington, IL 61704
United States
Phone: 309-665-0130
Fax: 720-367-3036
Web site: www.brownkraftlabels.com

For those of you unable to order labels in larger quantities, you may purchase individual

labels by the sheet. This company has great customer service and prompt delivery.

Online Labels
925 Florida Central Parkway
Longwood, FL 32750 USA
Toll Free: 1-888-575-2235
Florida: 407-949-6499
Fax: 1-866-406-7341
Web site: www.onlinelabels.com

If you're looking for a professional print job for short run labels, and you can't quite

afford to invest in a professional printer, then check out this company:

Primera Technology, Inc.
Two Carlson Parkway North
Plymouth, MN 55447-4446
USA
Phone: (763) 475-6676
Toll-Free: 1-800-797-2772
Fax: (763) 475-6677
Web site: www.primera.com

If you are ordering in bulk, Primera would be the ideal company to order from. Shipping
is very inexpensive and delivery is always prompt. They have over thirty different types
of label material to choose from. This company also offers a very *nice* high quality
printer to print professional labels both for your business and private labeling.

Lightning Labels
2369 S. Trenton Way, Unit C
Denver, Colorado 80231
Phone: 303.695.0398
Toll-Free: 888.685.2235
Fax: 303.6955.0441
Web site: **www.lightninglabels.com**

When you're ready to go professional and can't keep up with printing your own labels, allow the above company to do it for you. They offer competitive rates.

Stock Photo Web Sites

When it comes time to design your web site, you may find an interest in blending stock photography in with your own pictures of your products. Check out these sites:

Big Stock Photo
www.bigstockphoto.com

Download ROYALTY-FREE stock photos for $1-$2 per image. Choose from over 1,507,000 photos. This is one of my #1 websites for stock photography.

Getty Images
www.gettyimages.com

Very nice images, but somewhat expensive.

iStockPhoto
www.istockphoto.com

Royalty-free images ranging from $1-$15 depending on what size, and video clips from $10-$50 also based on size.

Foto Search Stock Photography and Stock Footage
www.fotosearch.com

Search from over 2 million images from over 100 stock photographs, stock illustrations, and video stock footage publishers at one website.

Label Factory Deluxe 2.0, 3.0 by Nova Development

This software can be found at any Staples, OfficeMax or Office Depot for around $29.95 or by clicking here: http://www.novadevelopment.com/Products/us/ldw/default.aspx. This software is awesome for round labels. I use it for a lot of things for my business and personal use.

Art Explosion Publisher Pro 2.0 by Nova Development

This software is absolutely *wonderful* in creating highly professional flyers, postcards, and business forms. I highly recommend this. Again, it can be purchased at any Staples, OfficeMax, Office Depot and Best Buy or by clicking here:

http://www.novadevelopment.com/products/us/pgw/default.aspx.

Other software you can use are things like Microsoft Word, Publisher, and CorelDraw.

WARNING LABELS

It is imperative to always have a warning label on every candle you give out. This provides information to your customer on how to properly burn soy candles. The disclaimer also provides product liability for your business.

I recommend having the following information on your labels:

WARNING:
Natural Burning Candles
To Prevent Fire or Personal Injury,
burn candle within sight and out of reach of
children and pets. Never burn candle on or near
anything that can catch fire. Keep wick centered &
trimmed to no more than 1/4 inch at all times to
prevent excessive flame & smoke.
Allow soy wax candle to burn for three
hours on the first burn to ensure an even
burn to the wax, and to prevent a
tunneling effect.

When you are completely comfortable taking your hobby to the next level by starting a business, I recommend adding your business information to your warning labels. This provides another form in advertising your business. But we will discuss that further in **Chapter 13: Turning Your Soy Candle Hobby into a Money-Making Venture!**

Here are other examples of warning labels that include business information:

WARNING:
Natural Burning Candles
To Prevent Fire or Personal Injury,
burn candle within sight and out of reach of
children and pets. Never burn candle on or near
anything that can catch fire. Keep wick centered &
trimmed to no more than 1/4 inch at all times to
prevent excessive flame & smoke.

YOUR BUSINESS NAME
www.yourbusinessname.com

Allow soy wax candle to burn for three hours on
the first burn to ensure an even burn to the wax.
If the candle doesn't burn for a minimum of three hours,
this can cause a tunneling effect.

8 oz.

WARNING:
Natural Burning Candles
To Prevent Fire or Personal Injury,
burn candle within sight and out of reach of
children and pets. Never burn candle on or near
anything that can catch fire. Keep wick centered &
trimmed to no more than 1/4 inch at all times to
prevent excessive flame & smoke.

Fragrance Name
YOUR BUSINESS NAME
www.yourbusinessname.com
(123) 456-7890

Allow soy wax candle to burn for three hours on
the first burn to ensure an even burn to the wax.
If the candle doesn't burn for a minimum of three hours,
this can cause a tunneling effect.

16 oz.

WARNING:
Natural Burning Candles
<u>**To Prevent Fire or Personal Injury,**</u>
burn candle within sight and out of reach of
children and pets. Never burn candle on or near
anything that can catch fire. Keep wick centered &
trimmed to no more than 1/4 inch at all times to
prevent excessive flame & smoke.
Allow soy wax candle to burn for three hours on
the first burn to ensure an even burn to the wax.
If the candle doesn't burn for a minimum of three hours
this can cause a tunneling effect.

<u>FRAGRANCE NAME</u>

4 oz.

<u>FRAGRANCE NAME</u>
<u>YOUR BUSINESS NAME</u>
<u>www.yourbusinessname.com</u>

WARNING:
Natural Burning Candles
<u>**To Prevent Fire or Personal Injury,**</u>
burn candle within sight and out of reach of
children and pets. Never burn candle on or near
anything that can catch fire. Keep wick centered &
trimmed to no more than 1/4 inch at all times to
prevent excessive flame & smoke.
Allow soy wax candle to burn for three hours on
the first burn to ensure an even burn to the wax.
If the candle doesn't burn for a minimum of thre hours
this can cause a tunneling effect.

10 oz.

WARNING:
Natural Burning Candles
<u>**To Prevent Fire or Personal Injury,**</u>
burn candle within sight and out of reach of
children and pets. Never burn candle on or near
anything that can catch fire. Keep wick centered &
trimmed to no more than 1/4 inch at all times to
prevent excessive flame & smoke.
Allow soy wax candle to burn for three hours on
the first burn to ensure an even burn to the wax.
If the candle doesn't burn for a minimum of three hours
this can cause a tunneling effect.

2 oz.

Chapter 10: Troubleshooting

Troubleshooting for Container & Molded Candles

Problem	Solution
There are lines inside the glass.	▪ The glass wasn't heated prior to pouring wax.
The candle surface has bubbles.	▪ The wax was too hot. ▪ The wax was poured too quickly. ▪ The wax temperature was too cool when poured. ▪ Use your heat gun or blow dryer to remove bubbles.
When burning, the flame burns in a tunnel down the center of candle.	▪ The wick is too small. Ensure that you use the proper size wick based on the diameter of the container. Size up or down or add an additional wick. ▪ Candle didn't properly burn for one hour for every inch in diameter of container.
Chalky frosting on surface of candle.	▪ Candle sat in a room temperature area and then was placed in a much cooler area. Soy candles are very sensitive in extreme heat and cold temperatures. You can re-melt candle by placing inside an oven or using a heat gun.
The wick is smoking excessively.	▪ The wick needs to be trimmed. Keep wick trimmed to ¼ inch. ▪ The wick is too large.
The wick has a very small flame or drowns in melted wax.	▪ The wick is too small and will not consume the melted wax. ▪ Too much fragrance oil and some dyes can clog the wicks.
Wick has moved after pouring wax.	▪ Make sure you secure your wick to the base of the container, using a Glue Dot™. If the wax is too hot, this will cause the Glue Dot™ to not adhere to the container.
The candle won't release from mold.	▪ The mold could have dents in it. ▪ The wax may not have completely cooled down. Allow candle to completely cool for at least twenty-four hours. ▪ The well was overfilled when topped off to fill sink holes. Be sure not to go above the previous pour.

Chapter 11: Additional Resources

Glossary of Candle Making Terms

Candle	Illuminating device made of a fiber wick enclosed in a cylinder of wax or fatty material.
Cold Scent Throw	How well a soy candle smells when the wick hasn't been lighted.
Cure Time	Means to age product. With age the fragrances become stronger, due to molecular structure changes of soy wax that can't be seen with a naked eye. Typical cure time for soy wax is two weeks.
Dipping Vat or Can	This is an aluminum can for over dipping your pillar candles.
Double Boiler	Pan placed inside a pot of water.
Flash Point for Fragrance Oils	The temperature the oil has to reach to catch fire when it comes in contact with a spark or open flame.
Flash Point for Soy Wax	Temperature the wax would have to reach before it combusts and catches fire.
Fractionated Coconut Oil	Made by pressing the coconut meat (copra). Aids in strengthening fragrance throw in candles.
Fragrance Oils	Synthetic and natural essential oil blends that create scented oil for candles and body care usage.
Frosting	White or chalky appearances on soy candles.
Glue Dots™	Used to secure wick to container.
Hot Scent Throw	How well a soy candle smells when burning.
Melt Pool	The size of melted wax that forms around the wick when candle is burning.
Melting Pitcher	Aluminum pot used to melt wax.
Melting Point	Temperature soy wax reaches when it melts. Soy wax blends come in several different melting points.
Mold Release	Powder or spray used to aid in the release of your soy candle from aluminum molds.
Mold Sealer	Usually available in grey or white putty, used to spread around the wick on the outside to prevent wax leakage.
Molds	Aluminum or polyurethane molds used to make freestanding candles. These come in a wide variety of shapes and sizes.

Mushrooming	Carbon buildup that forms on the tip of wicks, caused by incomplete combustion. The type of wicks used, additives and some fragrance oils can cause this.
Pouring Temperature	Temperature at which you pour your soy wax into your mold or containers. Pouring temperature varies depending on the type of soy wax you're using.
Relief Holes	Holes poked into wax to release air bubbles before re-pour.
Re-pour	Refilling container or mold where shrinkage has occurred, to level out.
Soot	Black residue commonly found on jars when proper candle care isn't maintained..
Soybean Wax	A renewable and environmentally preferable alternative to non-renewable petroleum wax. Soybean wax is safe and non-toxic and can easily be extracted for efficient recycling.
UV Inhibitor/Color Stabilizer	Available in a powder form. Used to inhibit color fading from exposure to UVA and UVB light by absorbing the light. Also prevents discoloration.
Wax Melter	Professional machine used to melt large amounts of wax at a time.
Wet Spots	Sections where wax pulls away from glass container.
Wick Tabs	Small, flat metal discs with a hole in the middle to secure wick. Used to hold wick in place at bottom of candle.

Chapter 12: Using Essential Oils in Soy Candles

WHAT IS AROMATHERAPY?

Aromatherapy is the practicing of using natural essences in promoting the well-being of your body, emotions, mind and good health. The essences used are called essential oils. Using pure, undiluted essential oils is the key to aromatherapy. It is said the ancient Egyptians were one of the first cultures to begin using plants for aromatic purposes.

Aromatherapy can help reduce stress, manage emotions and improve overall well-being. It is a holistic alternative to medicine and offers many easy ways to enhance the quality of your life and improve your health. Aromatherapy allows you, your family, and your customers to connect with nature. In such a fast-paced world, we have lost focus on the natural essences nature provides us. These scents have been proven for centuries to aid in many health ailments, reduce everyday stress, and promote wellness.

BENEFITS OF ESSENTIAL OILS

Essential oils are extracted from botanical plants, bark, leaves, stalks, seeds, roots and resins. Pure essential oils are highly concentrated and sometimes are called volatile oils because they evaporate when exposed to the air. Essential oils do not dissolve well in water but are soluble in vegetable oils and partially soluble in alcohol.

The benefits of essential oils can be achieved at several different levels. One of the first ways they affect people is through the sense of smell, which is the most sensitive of the five senses. Smells gain direct access to emotions. Another use of essential oils is through your skin, by stimulating circulation to surface skin cells and encouraging cell regeneration through the formation of new skin cells. Essential oils help relieve muscle tension such as spasms, as well as soothe sore muscles and calm inflamed or irritated skin. Your skin easily absorbs the molecules of essential oils so they can travel to the intercellular fluid surrounding the skin cells. The oils can help to boost your immune system by aiding in stimulating the body's own defense system, which encourages the production of white blood cells.

DOS & DON'TS

- **DO** use pure undiluted essential oils from a reliable supplier (see my recommendations).
- **DON'T** inhale essential oils directly from the bottle as this can burn your nasal passage.
- **DO** research which essential oils blend well together.
- **DON'T** open or pour essentials oils around a fire, stove or any other related heat source.
- **DO** be aware of your selection of essential oils as some can really be expensive for just a 1 oz. bottle. Stay away from these as it will cost you too much to manufacture.

AROMATHERAPY CANDLE PROJECTS

This is one of the most sought-after sections in the book! I have been asked many times how to make soy candles using essential oils. Well, after a year of research and testing I am sharing my secrets with you. Selling aromatherapy soy candles will yield a much higher profit due to the costs of producing a natural candle. It's important to make sure your marketing materials clearly identify your soy candles as being aromatherapy with pure essential oils.

PROJECT #1: ANOINTING SOY CANDLE

Materials Needed: GB 464 Soy Wax
Thermometer
Dye Chips
Frankincense Essential Oil
Myrrh Essential Oil
16 oz. Apothecary Jar
Eco 6 – Double Wick
Wick Bars or Clothesline clips
Aluminum Melting Pitcher

Follow the below steps:

Step 1: Wipe out any dust or residue you may see in your containers with either a towel or paper towels. Secure your wick using a Glue Dot™.

Step 2: Scoop out soy wax using an aluminum pouring pot. You do not have to worry about measuring the wax until it has completely melted. Set your electric hot plate on medium and allow wax to melt to 185°F. While your wax is melting, heat your container using a heat gun, blow dryer, or oven. Again, heating your jars will reduce or eliminate wet spots. Remember, this is not required, but highly recommended for best results.

Step 3: Once your wax has melted, use your thermometer to check the temperature. When your temperature has reached 185°F, remove from the heat source. Place an empty pouring pot on your digital scale and pour 16 oz. (1 lb) of wax. Weigh out ¼ oz. each of frankincense and myrrh essential oils. Stir well for at least two minutes until oil has blended into wax.

Note: ½ oz. of essential oil will suffice for 1 lb. of wax. Remember, essential oils are highly concentrated and are volatile oils. You will not use the same amount as you would of fragrance oils. Stir essential oil well to blend and bind into wax. Allow soy wax to cool to around 125°F.

Step 4: Now that your wax has cooled down to 125°F, it's time to pour. Slowly pour the wax into the container, straighten the wick, and secure it with a wick bar or clothesline clips. Clothesline clips are very inexpensive and highly recommended for beginners making candles. These can be found at Wal-Mart for about $3 for 100 or more.

Step 5: For best results, candles made with essential oils should cool at room temperature and be allowed to cure for up to ten days. This allows the essential oil to strengthen and aids in achieving a good scent throw.

Step 6: Trim wick to ¼ inch before lighting. Remember to do this each time you light your candle. Wipe your candle jar using Windex® to remove any waxy residue or greasy handprints.

You have now made your first aromatherapy candle! Remember to place the appropriate labels on your candles.

PROJECT #2: **COMFORT SOY CANDLE**

Materials Needed: GB 464 Soy Wax
Thermometer
Lavender Essential Oil
Chamomile Essential Oil
8 oz. Travel Tin
Eco 12
Wick Bars or Clothesline Clips
Aluminum Melting Pitcher

Follow the steps below:

Step 1: Wipe out any dust or residue you may see in your containers with either a towel or paper towels. Secure your wick using a Glue Dot™.

Step 2: Scoop out soy wax using aluminum pouring pot. You do not have to worry about measuring the wax until it has completely melted. Set your electric hot plate on medium and allow wax to melt to 185°F. While your wax is melting, heat your container with a heat gun, blow dryer or oven. Again, heating your jars will reduce or eliminate wet spots. Remember, this is not required but highly recommended for best results.

Step 3: Once your wax has melted, use your thermometer to check the temperature. When your temperature has reached 185°F remove from the heat source. Place an empty pouring pot on your digital scale and pour 16 oz. (1 lb) of wax. Weigh out ¼ oz. each of lavender and chamomile essential oils. Stir well for at least two minutes until oil has blended into wax.

Note: 1/2 oz. of essential oil will suffice for one pound of wax. Remember, essential oils are highly concentrated and are volatile oils. You will not use the same amount as you would of fragrance oils. Stir essential oil well to blend and bind into wax. Allow soy wax to cool to around 125°F.

Step 4: Now that your wax has cooled down to 125°F, it's time to pour. Slowly pour the wax into the container, straighten the wick, and secure it with a wick bar or clothesline clips. Clothesline clips are very inexpensive and highly recommended for beginners making candles or you can use metal wick bars found at Candle Science.

Step 5: For best results, candles made with essential oils should cool at room temperature and be allowed to cure for ten days. This allows the essential oil to strengthen and aids in achieving a good scent throw.

Step 6: Trim wick to ¼ inch before lighting. Remember to do this each time you light your candle. Wipe your candle jar using Windex® to remove any waxy residue or greasy handprints.

Step 7: Sprinkle some lavender buds as a finishing touch. Remember to place the appropriate labels on your candles.

PROJECT #3: BREATHE FREELY SOY CANDLE

Materials Needed:
GB 464 Soy Wax
Thermometer
Eucalyptus Essential Oil
Peppermint Essential Oil
Spearmint Essential Oil
15 oz. Cylinder
Eco 6 – Double Wick
Wick Bars or Clothesline clips
Aluminum Melting Pitcher

Follow the below steps:

Step 1: Wipe out any dust or residue you may see in your containers with either a towel or paper towels. Secure your wick using a Glue Dot™.

Step 2: Scoop out soy wax using an aluminum pouring pot. You do not have to worry about measuring the wax until it has completely melted. Set your electric hot plate on medium and allow wax to melt to 185°F. While your wax is melting, heat your container using a heat gun, blow dryer or oven. Again, heating your jars will reduce or eliminate wet spots. Remember, this is not required but highly recommended for best results.

Step 3: Once your wax has melted, use your thermometer to check the temperature. When your temperature has reached 185°F, remove from the heat source. Place an empty pouring pot on your digital scale and pour 16 oz. (1 lb) of wax. Weigh out ⅓ oz. each of eucalyptus, peppermint and spearmint essential oils. Stir well for at least two minutes until oil has blended into wax.

Note: ½ oz. of essential oil will scent one pound of wax. Remember, essential oils are highly concentrated and are volatile oils. You will not use the same amount as you would of fragrance oils. Stir essential oil well to blend and bind into wax. Allow soy wax to cool to around 125°F.

Step 4: Now that your wax has cooled down to 125°F, it's time to pour. Slowly pour the wax into the container, straighten the wick, and secure it with a wick bar or clothesline clips. Clothesline clips are very inexpensive and highly recommended for beginners making candles. These can be found at Wal-Mart for about $3 for 100 or more.

Step 5: For best results, candles made with essential oils should cool at room temperature and be allowed to cure for ten days. This allows the essential oil to strengthen and aids in achieving a good scent throw.

Step 6: Trim wick to ¼ inch before lighting. Remember to do this each time you light your candle. Wipe your candle jar using Windex® to remove any waxy residue or greasy handprints.

CREATE YOUR OWN AROMATHERAPY BLEND

As previously discussed in earlier pages, creating your own unique blend will give you a niche over your competitors.

Here are a few suggestions on essential oil blends:

A Little of this	And Some of this	To Get
Vanilla	Sandalwood	Aphrodisiac
Lavender	Vanilla	Passion
Sweet Orange	Grapefruit	Citrus
Lavender	Roman Chamomile	Relaxation
Ylang Ylang	Clary Sage	Clarity
Cedarwood	Spruce and Fir Needle	Deep Forest
Ginger	Sweet Orange	Spicy
Ylang Ylang and Patchouli	Sandalwood	Sensual Moments
Peppermint and Eucalyptus	Rosemary	True Breeze
Lemongrass	Bergamot	Stimulate
Tangerine and Sweet Orange	Lemon	Citrus Tangy Blend

Here are a few suggestions on fragrance oils (FO) and essential oil (EO) blends:

A Little of this	And Some of this	To Get
Sweet Orange EO	Almond FO	Paradise
Sandalwood EO	Vanilla Musk FO	Sentimental
Lavender EO	Chamomile Tea FO	Lavender Chamomile Tea
Bergamot EO	Lemongrass FO	Uplift
Lavender EO	Orange FO	Stress Less
Rosemary and Eucalyptus EO	Spearmint FO	Breathe Freely

Chapter 13: Packaging & Shipping Soy Candles

Once you have mastered your technique in making soy candles and all of the appropriate warning labels are affixed to your product there is one last, yet important, step: packaging your product and shipping it. The presentation of your soy candles is an important factor when it is time to market to the public. There are many cost effective ways to complete your finished product.

Now that you have a beautiful soy candle, it's important to put your name on it. I suggest having a professional graphic designer design your labels: it shouldn't cost more than a nominal fee of $25-$100. Your artwork can be printed on clear, white or kraft (brown) labels and I would suggest trying all different versions to see which would look best. Decide whether you would like to add a gift box to place your soy candle in, as this will change your price point to a higher perceived value. But also be mindful that you will have to produce more labels—one or possibly two for the box and one for the candle. I recommend doing your research to see what other candle companies have done in labeling to give you ideas as well as putting a twist on your own. I have found that circular or square labels look really great on candle jars such as apothecary, cylinder, travel tins and many more.

Shipping Soy Candles

Shipping your soy candles can be a daunting task and it definitely was difficult for me in the earlier days of candle making. Your shipping techniques will differ depending on whether you are shipping wholesale or to a retail (e-commerce) customer.

When shipping during the summer months, it's important to make sure the candles are sitting upright and you may have to insulate them with dry ice to prevent melting. But due to the changes to soy wax over the years, the melt points have increased, which definitely helps to avoid melting during the warmer months. Here's a reminder of the melt points for the soy waxes I recommend in this book:

- Golden Brands 464 – 115-119°F
- EcoSoya 135 - 122°F

RETAIL

When shipping to your retail customers, you can simply wrap your candles in bubble wrap and sit the candles upright in the box. I recommend using the water-soluble peanuts because this will confirm you are truly an eco-friendly company. It is important to make sure you place the peanuts at the bottom of the box then place your products in the center of the box and then fill the rest of the space with peanuts. Place the customer's invoice on top or somewhere in the box. One thing that I did to add a "wow factor" was to add a bit of fragrance oil to a few peanuts. When the customer opens up the box they are like, "Wow, this smells really great!"

WHOLESALE

Shipping your products to your wholesale clients will be a bit different from shipping to your retail customers simply because you are shipping bulk products. I'm big on recycling, so when I receive my glass containers from my suppliers, I simply reuse those boxes to package my wholesale clients' orders and I then place the box into a bigger box when I ship out. It's important to find a box that will have enough space around all sides so you can have peanuts at the bottom and all around to prevent breakage. You can order brown shipping boxes and shipping supplies from Uline.com.

Always remember to have "FRAGILE" or "HANDLE WITH CARE" labels placed on all of your packages. This will not prevent damage but hopefully the people handling the package will be more careful.

SHIPPING SUPPLIES

Supplies	Where to Buy
Brown shipping boxes, packaging tape, water-soluble peanuts, fragile labels, invoice package slip, bubble wrap, gift boxes, corrugated rolls of paper, scales	www.uline.com, www.fetpak.com, www.papermart.com, www.packagingsupplies.com, www.shippingsupply.com, www.ebay.com, www.esupplystore.com, www.usps.com

SHIPPING CARRIERS

USPS - If you decide to ship via United States Postal Service (USPS) you may order *free* boxes by going to their website. When you're just starting your business, this will be the best route to take. USPS now offers varying sizes on flat rate shipping which is a *big* plus! Be sure to print your shipping labels online on their website as this will save you time and a few cents.

FEDEX – When comparing rates from UPS to FedEx, I have found that FedEx is the least expensive of the carriers based on weight. However, in my opinion their service is not the best. Having worked for this company several years ago, I saw firsthand how packages were being handled by the workers. They would throw packages off of the belts which were at least three to five feet from the floor; the persons would throw packages into their trucks and simply just being careless. Unfortunately, there aren't many choices out there when shipping your product(s).

UPS – "What can brown do for you?" UPS is another common carrier. Again, in my opinion, their services aren't any better. I highly recommend insuring your package(s) to ensure you and your customers are covered. I have found UPS pricing to be much higher than FedEx.

Chapter 14: Turning Your Soy Candle Hobby into a Money-Making Venture!

Five Reasons to Make Candles

- It's really easy and exciting to do!
- The feeling you get when someone wants to purchase a natural soy candle that you made by hand.
- You will cultivate new friendships.
- It's really inexpensive to get started and the benefits are very rewarding.
- This is an excellent way to bring in another source of income.
- You are in control of your destiny.

When I decided to go further with candle making, turning my hobby into a business was very important. At the time I started, I wasn't making a lot of money but also wanted more out of my life. I began taking my candles to my job to see what my co-workers thought. To my surprise, they loved my candles! From that moment on, I knew I was on to something and it was just a matter of perfecting my craft.

I spent the next several months sharpening my candle-making skills and selling my creations in the process. Fortunately, I have an artistic background which I was able to apply to my candle designs. Don't let this scare you away if you are not artistically talented because you will have other talents you can incorporate into your candles.

Over the years, I've realized the candle market is saturated and that means you have to do research to see what everyone else is doing, both with large and small candle companies. From there you will be able to find your niche. The idea is to take what is current and make it better, or be the first to create something unique.

IS THE CANDLE BUSINESS RIGHT FOR YOU?

Prior to moving forward with your business, I recommend evaluating your current status in your life and answer the questions below:

1. How much time are you willing to devote to your new business?

2. Are you willing to devote late night hours or early morning hours in the beginning stages to build your business?

3. What are you trying to accomplish with your business?

4. What is your motivation for starting your new business?

5. Do you have family or friends who would have an interest in participating or helping with your new candle business?

SETTING GOALS

It's important to have your day planned out when you get up each day. It is easy to lose focus of your tasks. I am so guilty of this. There have been times when I mentally had set out to do certain things throughout the day, but due to whatever reasons I always lost track of the important tasks. By the end of the day I would be completely exhausted and didn't feel a sense of having completed anything. There were times when I spent too much time on one task, which prevented me from doing anything else.

A very good friend who saw my frustration suggested I write out a "to do" list each night for the next day. Not only did she recommend the "to do" list but, she also suggested allotting times to each specific task. Although I thought this was going to be a headache and not necessary, to my surprise it turned out to be the best thing I could have ever done for myself. Amazingly, I had always written out a "to do" list for my day jobs, but not once did I think to apply that same concept to my business. After my first week of writing out my list each day, not only did I accomplish my tasks, but I finally learned how to manage working full-time, caring for a family, and building my home-based business. Granted, at times it's not easy but with dedication it will work and be the best thing for you, as it was for me.

When writing out your overall goals and devising your plan, it's important to follow the SMART acronym:

- Specific
- Measurable
- Attainable
- Relevant
- Time-Bound

Setting goals is not a complicated process, nor is it time consuming. It can be as simple or as complicated as you make it to be. Set your goals to push yourself beyond what you feel you're capable of accomplishing. For example, if you have been making $100 a day selling your products then set your goal to make $200 per day. Making $200 per day is easily attainable if you sell ten 16 oz. candles for $20, or if you sell the candles for $10, then all you need to sell is twenty candles.

Dos & Don'ts

So where should you begin prior to starting your business? Start by creating your ultimate dream plan to fulfill your business goals. If you don't have a plan, how can you know where you're going? I honestly didn't start out with a plan and spent years making lots of financial mistakes.

View the list of dos and don'ts below:

- **DO** create your ultimate entrepreneurial dream plan–this should include what types of candle containers you want to carry, how many different size containers, whether you want to provide dye free or dyed candles, fragrance or essential oil choices, if you want a theme, etc.

- **DON'T** get overwhelmed trying to carry every fragrance, every container or every color…you will go *broke* really fast!

- **DO** get advice from close family and friends and even other candle makers. This will aid by having someone else help you to focus and narrow your ideas.

- **DON'T** rush out to order lots of supplies until you know the direction of your business.

- **DO** spend time creating your business name and logo. Research inexpensive options or barter to have graphic work done. Creating a professional image is the key to your business success! When deciding on a business name, check to see if the domain name is available on the Internet. It would be terrible to have settled on a business name and then have the domain name unavailable.

- **DON'T** attempt to pay for every service you need for your business. For example, if you need your website, brochures, and such designed for your business, attempt to barter your services prior to paying. Always negotiate rates.

TOP THREE MISTAKES TO AVOID:

MISTAKE #1 – Ordering a little of this and a little of that!

If you don't have a well thought out plan for how you want to operate your business as far as what fragrances you want to carry and type of containers you will have, you can end up spending a lot of money that will go down the drain.

When I first started, I wanted to carry every fragrance I smelled, not realizing I needed to have every last one of those fragrances in stock when a customer ordered it. Well, if you don't have the financial resources to take out loans or charge credit cards, then trying to keep over fifty fragrances in stock will be a challenge.

Write down how many fragrances you want to carry and which scents they should be. I recommend carrying no more than five fragrances in the beginning. This will enable you to buy in larger quantities and you will save a bundle on shipping fees.

This also applies to what type of candle containers you want to carry. To get an idea of what's selling in your area, I suggest taking a trip out to your local mall and craft fairs to see what others are selling. If what they're selling works for them and is making money, then why reinvent the wheel? You can decide whether you want to carry the same container styles your competitors are carrying and simply adjust your pricing or select better styles and offer the same and/or different fragrances. You should carry no more than two to three different types of containers in the beginning, perhaps small, medium and large.

MISTAKE #2 - Trying to be everything to everybody

When I got into candle making it took four or five years to wake up and realize I could not be everything to everybody. I tried to accommodate each of my customers by custom designing candles specifically to what they wanted. If I didn't have a particular fragrance then I would order it. *This is a big no no!* I have found that you could carry over 100 different fragrances and if a customer couldn't find something they like out of those hundred fragrances then nine times out of ten they wouldn't have bought from you if you carried 175 fragrances. I can't tell you how many people I have talked to for ten to twenty minutes when they didn't buy anything at all and yet our conversation was simply about fragrances, the ones I have and the ones they think I should carry.

MISTAKE #3 – Using too many suppliers

Whew!! I couldn't tell you how many suppliers I worked with in the beginning. I had at least six suppliers for fragrances, three to four for containers, and the list goes on. I went through so much stress trying to keep up with where I ordered what. I was buying supplies from companies on the West Coast (I live on the East Coast) and there were suppliers who were very competitive in pricing on my side of the world. Limiting your suppliers can save you a ton in shipping fees. You want to be able to find suppliers that:

- are close to you
- offer free samples or samples at a very low cost (especially on fragrances)
- offer all or most of the products you need
- offer a variety of shipping methods at affordable rates
- offer no or very low minimum orders
- have a return policy you agree with
- carry undiluted fragrances oil

Chapter 15: The Business Side

Register Your Business

Once you have decided to turn your hobby into a business, there is some important information you should you know. Starting your business requires a series of steps and right decisions. You have to decide on a business name and type of ownership and you have to obtain your licenses.

Business Name

Your business name is very important! It should speak to what type of products you are selling. It is important to check your local state's office to see if your business name is already taken and, depending on the type of ownership, there may be additional legal requirements. More information can be found at this website: http://www.sba.gov/smallbusinessplanner/start/nameyourbusiness/index.html. You can check out your local states requirements at this website: http://www.statelocalgov.net/50states-secretary-state.cfm.

Types of Ownership

Sole Proprietorships – Firms owned by one person; sole proprietors own all assets to the business and assume full responsibility for all debts and liabilities.

Partnerships – Two or more people have ownership.

Corporations – Shareholders are the owners of the corporation. When ownership changes, the corporation does not dissolve.

S Corporations – This is another form of a corporation; this structure is taxed differently.

Limited Liability Corporation (LLC) – This has characteristics of both a corporation and partnership; the owners have limited liability for the actions and debts of the company.

Licenses

Most business types, with the exception of sole proprietors, must apply for a federal Employee ID Number (EIN) regardless of whether the company has employees or not. It is so easy to obtain your EIN via the IRS website. The application can be submitted online and you will receive a temporary EIN. Go to:

http://www.irs.gov/businesses/index.html.

Most states require business registration for the sole purposes of taxes and basic business functions. Because your candle business will be engaging in sales, if your state has income tax you will need to register with the Department of Revenue or Treasury for a state certification number. Check your local state government's website for more information.

Insurance

At the time of starting your business, it's very important to make sure you have insurance to protect you against any accidents. There are several types of insurance you may need for your business:

Product Liability – This insurance protects your business from claims related to the manufacturing and selling of products to the public. The insurance will cover the manufacturer's or seller's liability against any losses or injuries to the buyer.

Home-Based Business – This insurance covers all the business-related equipment in your home. Many people think their homeowner's insurance will cover their business needs–it will not! Homeowner's insurance will only cover possessions related to your home and not your business.

General Liability – This insurance covers real or alleged bodily injury, personal injury and property damage arising from your business operations. For example, if your sibling comes to your house just to visit and slips and falls, this will not be covered. But if your customer comes to your home and slips and falls, it will be covered.

Here is a list of insurance companies that we found offering small business insurance,

Benchmark Insurance
111 Hoff Road Westerville, Ohio 43086
Phone: (614) 891-7791

Bob Bowers
Bowers and Associates
Corning, NY
Phone: (607) 962-6596

Capitol Indemnity Corp.
4610 University Avenue
P.O. Box 5900
Madison, Wisconsin 53705-0900

Co-operative Insurance Companies
P.O. Box 5890
Middlebury, VT 05753
Toll Free: (800) 639-4017
http://www.co-opinsurance.com

Hays Insurance Agency
Jackie Hays
507 E. Brazos Ave.
West Columbia, TX 77486
Phone: (979) 345-2271

Masters & Associates Insurance
P.O. Box 148
Miamisburg, Ohio 45342-0148
Phone: (937) 866-3361

State Farm Insurance
www.statefarm.com

Wachovia Bank
http://www.wachovia.com/small_biz

Trademarks, Copyrights & Patents

What is a Patent?

A patent for an invention is the grant of a property right to the inventor, issued by the

United States Patent and Trademark Office. Generally, the term of a new patent is twenty

years from the date on which the application for the patent was filed in the United States or, in special cases, from the date an earlier related application was filed, subject to the payment of maintenance fees. U.S. patent grants are effective only within the United States, U.S. territories, and U.S. possessions. Under certain circumstances, patent term extensions or adjustments may be available.

What Is a Trademark or Service Mark?

A trademark is a word, name, symbol, or device that is used in trade with goods to indicate the source of the goods and to distinguish them from the goods of others. A service mark is the same as a trademark except that it identifies and distinguishes the source of a service rather than a product. The terms "trademark" and "mark" are commonly used to refer to both trademarks and service marks.

Trademark rights may be used to prevent others from using a confusingly similar mark, but not to prevent others from making the same goods or from selling the same goods or services under a clearly different mark. Trademarks which are used in interstate or foreign commerce may be registered with the USPTO. The registration procedure for trademarks and general information concerning trademarks is described on a separate page entitled "Basic Facts about Trademarks" (http://www.uspto.gov/web/offices/tac/doc/basic/).

What Is a Copyright?

Copyright is a form of protection provided to the authors of "original works of authorship" including literary, dramatic, musical, artistic, and certain other intellectual works, both published and unpublished. The 1976 Copyright Act generally gives the owner of copyright the exclusive right to reproduce the copyrighted work, to prepare derivative works, to distribute copies or phonorecords of the copyrighted work, to perform the copyrighted work publicly, or to display the copyrighted work publicly.

The copyright protects the form of expression rather than the subject matter of the writing. For example, a description of a machine could be copyrighted, but this would only prevent others from copying the description; it would not prevent others from writing a description of their own or from making and using the machine. Copyrights are registered by the Copyright Office of the Library of Congress.

Information provided courtesy of the United States Patent and Trademark Office. More information can be found by visiting: http://www.uspto.gov/main/trademarks.htm.

E-commerce Shopping Carts

When just starting a business, many people rush out and purchase shopping carts for their websites. Often times, new owners have spent a lot of money on these ecommerce shopping carts. Do your research and carefully compare the shopping carts. In the beginning, the goal should be to keep your expenses as low as possible until your business takes off.

I would highly suggest www.mals-e.com as your shopping cart in the beginning until you're able to grow your business. Mals-e offers a *free* shopping cart as well as a premium shopping cart for $80 annually. Other great shopping carts are listed below:

www.checkout.google.com

www.godaddy.com/gdshop/ecommerce/cart.asp?ci=9042

www.oscommerce.com

www.paypal.com

www.volusion.com

www.x-cart.com

www.zen-cart.com

Payment Methods

Cash – This is always the best and quickest method of payment. When attending craft fairs, it's important to either have a cash box or a waist pouch to keep your cash close to you at all times. It's also important when preparing for shows to take a trip to the bank to have enough change on hand. Always keep a record of how much you started with so your accounting adds up at the end of the day. I typically keep a drawer of $100 total, broken out in fifty $1 bills, five $5 dollar bills, and three $10 dollar bills.

Checks – Accepting checks is another good payment method where no fees are incurred. The only problem to watch out for is bounced checks. In all my years of doing business I have never received a check that bounced. Below are some tips when accepting checks:

- Do not accept starting checks or checks with numbers less than 500.
- View the customer's driver's license or picture ID and verify the name, address and contact number match; if not, write it on the check.

- If you charge for returned checks, it is important to have this information posted at the point of sale.

Credit or Debit Cards − Many of you are aware that credit cards increase the consumers' spending because they can buy now and pay later. Accepting credit cards allows for better sales from customers all over the world. When choosing to accept credit cards, it is important to research the merchant's fees based on your credit card sale usage per month. The fees are based on the percentage of the total sale. Debit cards can be used like credit cards but these cards are linked to the customer's checking account and offer a much more convenient way of payment than writing checks. Below are a few merchants to check out:

www.authorize.net
www.charge.com
www.cardservicesales.com
www.godaddy.com/gdshop/ecommerce/landing.asp?ci=9041
www.paypal.com
www.propay.com
www.transact4free.com

Photographs

When you are just starting your business, there is no rush to have professional photographs of your products. I did not have professional pictures of my products until the beginning of 2008. To get started, you can take pictures using a digital camera. I purchased my first digital camera at www.ubid.com for around $149 plus shipping.

Fortunately, I had a little background knowledge of photography from learning various techniques in high school. To begin taking your own photographs you will need the following supplies:

- Four white foam boards
- Bright light
- Tripod
- Various props

All you will need to do is tape the foam boards together to make a back and two sides, and then put one at the bottom to place your products on. Having the right lighting and understanding the features of your camera is important.

Begin practicing with your camera and products against the background. If it's too much for you and you prefer to have professional photographs, below is a list of photographers who have experience in product photography or offer business photography packages:

Adobe Photographers Directory
Website: www.photographersdirectory.adobe.com/

This directory gives you swift access to contact information and allows you to view portfolios of photographers from around the world.

Erica Erck Photography
7617 Leveson Way
Nashville, TN 37211
Phone: 615-772-5528
Website: www.ericaerckphotography.com

Portrait Innovations
www.portraitinnovations.com
Portrait Innovations offer business packages to those wishing to have professional photographs. This is their most recent pricing guide:

You will receive:

- High quality prints
- High resolution CD of photographs

Three poses for $69.95

Six poses for $99.95

This pricing may vary depending on your location.

Product Photographers
www.productphotographers.net

This site will provide contact information and the ability to screen and hire photographers from around the globe. If you prefer to save money like myself, then I would recommend purchasing "photo studio in a box." These are the best kits for taking professional pictures of your products without having to spend thousands of dollars. There are many companies out there selling "photography in a box" from prices ranging from $57 to $300 plus. I purchased mine from eBay or you can check out these companies listed below:

Cubelite
www.cubelite.com
www.cubelite.co.uk

This company is quite expensive in what they offer. However, the products are excellent! I had an opportunity to meet with one of the sales representatives who took a picture of my candles and the results were amazing.

Discount Tommy
www.discounttommy.com/Shop/Control/fp/SFV/32282

I purchased my "photo studio in a box" from this company and I was quite pleased with what I received. After spending months shopping for the right price, I received a lot for my money through this company.

OBN Photography Equipment
www.obnphoto.com

This is another inexpensive company offering the "photo studio in a box." They have everything you need to have professional pictures of your products at an affordable price.

Chapter 16: Marketing Your Products

Marketing your product is very, very important and it is not an easy task. Marketing is the most important aspect of your business's success. You could have the worst product but the right marketing plan could have your product in the hands of almost every consumer.

When I first started selling my candles, I began taking samples to my job and showing them to various co-workers. After receiving orders, I began researching other ways to promote my business.

Craft Fairs

When I was ready to sell my candles I began selling at local craft fairs in Maryland, the District of Columbia, and Virginia. Usually around the holidays the schools hold various craft fairs to raise money for the schools and to enable small businesses to gain exposure.

The typical cost to exhibit at the craft fairs ranges from $25 to $75 for either an 8 x 8 or 10 x 10 space. The vendors typically provide one chair and a table. There are some things you should be aware of prior to paying your money to exhibit:

- Be careful exhibiting at craft fairs that are in their 1st year because you nor does the company have any idea of what the traffic will be like and don't believe them when they say they expect 100,000 people to show up. How will they know this if it's their first year?.

- Always find out the amount of attendees in past shows.

- Will you be indoors or outdoors?

- If outdoors, can you bring a tent or will a tent be provided?

Craft Fair on a Budget

During these tough economic times many of the small businesses have been drastically affected. However, there are many things you can do to keep the cost to a minimum when exhibiting at craft fairs. Here are some suggestions:

Share a Booth – It is important to first check with the vendor to see if booth sharing is allowed. If so, partner up with a friend or crafter selling products that differ from your business.

Bring Drinks & Food – Don't spend your profit by purchasing food at the location or ordering out. Pack sandwiches, bottled water and snacks. This keeps you at your booth at all times to meet your customers. Concession stands can be quite expensive. Don't blow your profit on eating.

Local Shows – Planning your craft fairs and remaining local will help keep your expenses low and enable you to exhibit at more shows throughout the year.

How Much Inventory to Bring

Knowing how much inventory to bring to a craft fair is one of the toughest decisions to make. You want to be able to bring enough to meet the demands of the number of customers attending but you don't want to have too much that doesn't sell. This was definitely an area that I struggled with often and learned the hard way. Although I would always sell a lot, I still made up too much.

I once attended a five day festival where the promoters stated over 100,000 people were planning to attend. So I decided to make up 1,600 candles. I sold 600 candles over the five day event but was left with 700 candles. Needless to say, a lot of candles ended up sitting around in storage.

My advice is that it's always best to sell out rather than taking product home. Determine how much you are going to bring based on the number of days for the craft fair and the number of attendees. If the craft fair has been taking place annually for several years then I would consider making up at least 100 candles per 20,000 people for a five day show or 75-100 candle s per day. It's best to sell out and take orders than taking product home with you. Also, determine how much profit you would like to make minus your expenses and that helps determine how much inventory you should bring.

Booth Etiquette

When attending craft shows, it's important to know good booth etiquette to make you a great neighbor. At times, we all get caught up in our own to do's when attending these fairs but we have to remember there are other crafters there trying to achieve the same results you are…to make money. Here are some suggestions:

Booth Space – If you paid for a 10 x 10 space then you need to keep all of your stuff within that space. Do not extend your display into your neighbor's space as this is the quickest way to create an exhibitor enemy. If you require additional space, buy it from the event promoter prior to the start of the show.

Setting up for the show – It is important to arrive at the times allotted to set up for your show. Be sure to allow yourself plenty of time to set up so you can be finished prior to customers arriving. Customers find it annoying when booths are not set up and the crafter is trying to sell products.

Be Friendly – It's true when they say, "you never know who you may meet." So be nice to the other exhibitors because you never know what their story is. I have met so many wonderful small business owners with years of experience exhibiting who provided me with a wealth of information. Be friendly, and don't be a pest.

Simply be aware of your surroundings and sit back and observe because you will learn a lot at each and every show. There are craft fairs and festivals held annually all over the world. You can use the following sources to find many exhibit opportunities (these descriptions are from their websites):

ART FAIR SOURCE BOOK
www.artfairsourcebook.com

The Definitive Guide to the Best Juried Art & Craft Fairs in the United States.

EVENT LISTER
www.eventlister.com

This website provides information on craft fairs and events throughout the United States.

FESTIVAL NETWORK ONLINE
www.festivalnetwork.com

This website is the ultimate online resource for music festivals, art and craft shows, home and garden shows, and specialty events. Providing extensive show details since 1996!

SOUTHERN FESTIVALS
www.southernfestivals.com

Southern Festivals lists festivals and events in the south, including North Carolina, South Carolina, Florida, Georgia, Louisiana, Tennessee, Texas and Virginia. Their features are informative articles on festivals, fairs, vendors and entertainers for the travel and tourism industry.

SUNSHINE ARTIST
www.sunshineartist.com

Sunshine Artist is the nation's leading publication for art and craft show exhibitors, promoters and patrons. Since 1972, SA has provided its readers with comprehensive reviews of everything from fine art fairs and festivals to small craft shows around the country, focusing on all aspects of the shows from sales to artist amenities, to the quality of art or craft.

Here are links to purchase craft fair equipment if necessary:

EZ-UP TENT SHELTERS
1601 Iowa Avenue
Riverside, California 92507
Toll Free: 800-45-SHADE
Fax: 951-781-0586
Website: http://www.ezup.com/index.html

SMART FURNITURE
430 Market Street.
Chattanooga, TN 37402
Toll Free: 888-GO-SMART (888-467-6278)
Website: http://www.smartfurniture.com/shop/retail.html

This company carries an extensive supply of shelving and displays for both retail stores and for trade show exhibitions. They also provide custom design collections to suit your business needs.

Trade Shows

Exhibiting at trade shows is a great way, if not the best way, to introduce your product to customers and prospects from around the world in a short amount of time. Trade shows not only give you the opportunity to showcase your product, but also allow you to give a first impression of your business.

At a typical national trade show, with 10,000 attendees and 1,000 exhibitors, you can realistically have 200 visitors per day. If you were making sales calls, you could not even approach that number. Granted, you don't always have the opportunity to go into as much detail in your presentation as you would like, but it opens the door for future communications—a door that sometimes is very difficult to get your foot into.

So for most companies, trade shows are worth the effort. In fact, before you decide to nix a show your company has attended for years, think about what that might say to your current customers who expect to see you there. This is especially damaging if your company has been through recent staffing or management changes, mergers, acquisitions, or other changes your clients may have heard about. Your competition will use your absence to their advantage. This doesn't mean you can't ever stop attending a show, but just be sure you think about whom you see there and what your company's absence may lead them to believe. If necessary, send a postcard to your primary clients who you know attend that particular show, and explain your decision to attend one particular show over another.

Before you even start looking for shows, you need to set your goals. To help you do this, there are four questions you need to ask yourself:

1. Why are you exhibiting?

    Are you trying to extend your relationship with existing customers? Introducing a new product? Positioning your company within the market? Generating qualified leads for new sales? Countering a competitor's claim?

2. Who is your target audience?

3. What is the message you want to convey?

4. What do you want to get out of the show?

   Do you want to bring home leads, sell your product/service, or

   create/improve/build upon your company image?

You need specific, measurable goals if you want your trade show activities to succeed.

SELECTING THE RIGHT SHOWS

When thinking about traveling to trade shows, your first thought is probably, "Okay, which shows are being held in Vegas?" However, with over 9,000 trade shows every year, you have to make your choices wisely to stretch your marketing dollar, because even though trade shows give you a great bang for the buck, they also cost quite a bit to attend. You and any booth staffers you hire (those are the people who stand in the booth to tell visitors about your business—and hopefully sell your products or services) may not want to go to Milwaukee in January, but if that's where the best show is, then that's where you have to send them. But which shows are the best shows?

The first place to start is with your industry's associations. These shows will typically be targeted right to your market, and often are reasonable in cost. You can also check with the trade publications you advertise in (or perhaps should be advertising in). Another resource is, of course, the web. Go to TSNN.com, tscentral.com, or FITA.org for directories of shows around the world in all types of industries. No list is entirely complete, however, so make sure you go to more than one directory.

DESIGNING YOUR BOOTH

There are lots of things to take into consideration when purchasing and designing your booth. These include the size and type of booth; that is, do you need a floor model or tabletop model? If you need a floor model, does it need to be a large custom booth to communicate the right corporate image, or will a smaller, more versatile floor model work? There is a huge variety of configurations for booths. You can have a large custom booth built that will require multiple booth spaces and a crew of workers to assemble, or you can opt for a smaller, ten foot (three meter) size that can be easily shipped and assembled and disassembled by you or your booth staffers. Often these smaller, modular versions can be broken down and used as two tabletop booths as well.

Here are the main things to think about when deciding what type of booth you need:

1. What are your functional needs for the booth?

    *   Do you need seating so you can sit and discuss at length with prospects the great benefits of your services or products? If your product or service is more complicated or technical, this functionality might work well for you.

    *   Do you need shelving for books or product displays, video capability, or storage?

    *   Do you need the booth to be easily assembled, disassembled and packed?

    *   Do you need to be able to reconfigure it for different shows or other uses?

    *   What kind of traffic flow do you need through your booth?

2. What are your aesthetic needs?

    *   Do you need a display with movement to illustrate your product?

- Does it need to be backlit to illustrate the detail of your product?

- Does your corporate image necessitate a certain "look" that would require curves, sharp/crisp lines, or colors?

3. What are your marketing needs?

- What is the message you need to communicate?

- Do you have strong name/logo recognition already?

- Are you a start-up trying to make a name for yourself?

4. What is your booth budget?

- Booth prices vary greatly depending on the size and format. Figure around $1,000 for a tabletop (graphics make a big difference in pricing), around the $5,000 to $15,000 range for a ten foot (three meter) portable with graphics, and for large 20 x 20 foot, 20 x 30 foot or 30 x 30 foot custom booths, the sky is the limit. (The rule of thumb is $92 to $120 per square foot, depending on the design.)

Article courtesy of: Obringer, Lee Ann. "How Trade Shows Work." '01 January, 2003. HowStuffWorks.com. <http://money.howstuffworks.com/trade-show.htm> 20 Januar,y 2009.

Once you've answered these questions, you should have a better idea of the type of booth you need, but the trickiest part of all is determining how the booth will look.

There is a host of well-known trade shows held annually and semi-annually throughout the United States. Below is a partial list of those shows and contact information for them:

Trade shows held at America's Mart in Atlanta, GA:

- The Atlanta Spring Gift, Home Furnishings & Holiday Market – usually held in March
- The Atlanta Spring Immediate Delivery Show – usually held in May
- Atlanta Gift & Home Furnishings Market – usually held in July and January

- Atlanta Fall Gift & Home Furnishings Market – usually held in September
- The Atlanta Fall Immediate Delivery Show – usually held in October

For more information, please contact:

AMC, Inc. / AmericasMart® Atlanta
240 Peachtree Street N.W., Suite 2200
Atlanta, GA 30303-1327
Website: www.americasmart.com

Trade shows held at the Jacob K. Javits Convention Center in New York:

- International Hotel/Motel & Restaurant Show
  www.javitscenter.com

- New York International Gift Fair
  www.javitscenter.com

- MJSA (Manufacturing Jewelers & Suppliers of America, Inc.)
  http://www.mjsainc.com

For more information, please contact:

Jacob K. Javits Convention Center
655 West 34th Street
New York, NY 10001-1188
Website: www.javitscenter.com

Trade shows held at the Las Vegas Convention Center in Las Vegas, NV:

- WWDMAGIC
  http://www.magiconline.com/magic/v42/index.cvn
  This is one of the largest and most recognized shows in the United States.

- International Restaurant Show
  www.lvcva.com

For more information, please contact:

Las Vegas Convention Center
3150 Paradise Road
Las Vegas, NV 89109
http://www.lvcva.com/

Trade shows held at the Moscone Convention Center in San Francisco, CA:

SFIGF – San Francisco International Gift Fair
http://www.moscone.com/site/do/index

For more information, please contact:

Moscone Convention Center
747 Howard Street
San Francisco, CA 94103
Website: www.moscone.com

Trade shows held at the Sands Expo and Convention Center in Las Vegas, NV

Natural MarketPlace
www.naturalproductsassoc.org/tradeshow

For more information, please contact:

Sands Expo and Convention Center
The Venetian Resort Hotel
Las Vegas, NV
www.naturalproductsassoc.org/tradeshow

More information on trade shows throughout the United States as well as internationally can be found at www.eventseye.com. Here you will find a comprehensive list of trade shows in every state, as well as international ones.

Internet

Another good and effective way to get notice to your new business is by creating a professional website to showcase your products and service. It's important when planning the design of your website to know what you want and how you want to display it. I highly recommend doing research prior to settling on a designer. When I first had a website designed for the candle business, I had hired this web designer who I thought was really good. Well, when he designed my site in the beginning I liked it, but visually it really wasn't what I wanted. Within a few months and after I'd wasted $1,200, I decided to have my website redesigned. I went through several designers until I found one who was able to create my visions with her twist.

Referrals

One of the best marketing tactics is still the same old fashion way—*word of mouth*. Have your friends and family try out your product and when they love it, they will end up telling their friends and their friends will tell their friends and so on.

Giving out free samples to people such as your children's teachers, and your co-workers is another good way to get folks to try your products and to get them to spread the word to others. Always keep your business cards on you at all times because you never know who you will meet.

Home Parties

Hosting home parties or getting someone else to host a party is another fun way to gain business exposure. Prior to having my website designed I had taken pictures of my candles and created a catalog. Within a couple of months, or maybe a few weeks, I started booking parties. My candle parties typically lasted for an hour and a half to two and a half hours and it was a fun way to help develop my selling techniques and meet new people, as well as a good way to make money and build my business.

I was about four months pregnant when I had my first candle party in Baltimore, Maryland. The hostess provided finger foods and drinks and I showed up with the products. After a two hour show, I tallied the sales and found I had made over $700. I was absolutely amazed! I rewarded the hostess with 15% of the total sales up to $499, and 20% for sales of $500 plus and she also received free products.

So how can you get started in home parties? It's simple! Create or have a catalog, brochure or sales sheet designed to showcase your candle products. Begin to distribute your marketing piece to anyone interested in your candles.

Independent Sales Reps

There are many advantages to hiring independent sales representatives to help take your product(s) to market, as well as some disadvantages. There are two different areas in which you can have independent sales reps: 1) sign up a specified number of consultants who will represent your company, and in return they will receive a percentage of the sales as well as company incentives. This choice typically involves signing up individuals who are looking to earn a supplemental income. 2) sign up professional sales representatives who have years of experience who sell for a living for various companies. These types of sales reps will promote your product to businesses who will order from you wholesale.

Over the years I have seen many candle companies start up by signing on sales reps and/or consultants to help launch and grow their business. As fast as I have seen these companies open, months later they closed due to poor planning. Many of these companies start their businesses by launching a consultant program allowing those interested in earning a supplemental income to join their company as a founder of the company with higher percentages and incentives, but they are required to purchase packages to get started. These types of companies are similar to being Multi-Level Marketing (MLM).

If you are serious about taking your candles to market then I highly recommend signing up professional sales representatives to promote your products. These sales reps either work for a sales company or self-employed but are full-time sales representatives. They are out there meeting with new clients and introducing new products to their existing clients. These folks are paid monthly with a 15% commission on all sales (industry standard). I have several representatives throughout the U.S. that promote our candles and our sales have ranged from $150 to as high as $1,200 for a single order. There are some advantages and disadvantages to working with sales reps.

ADVANTAGES

Experience – Professional sales representatives are experienced and successful in writing orders. They usually already have a large book of businesses they can pitch your business products to.

No Maintenance Expenses – You don't incur any maintenance expenses when you hire an independent sales rep. You do not have to pay for any travel expenses, phone services or any employment expenses.

DISADVANTAGES

No Commitment – The unfortunate side to being a new manufacturer is that your products are often at the bottom of the barrel unless your product is something that really stands out that will produce the money for the rep.

Competition – Unless you have a written contract with the rep stating otherwise, they will also promote lines that compete with your products.

When you are ready to hire independent sales representatives, you will need to supply them with a sales sheet, catalog or brochure of your products and samples of your candles. Keep in mind that if you offer a lot of fragrances, the sales rep will need samples of all fragrances to promote to their clients.

To locate independent sale representatives for your company, check out the websites below:
www.rephunter.net
www.replocate.com
www.mrpusa.com

Wholesale

Wholesale is selling your product in bulk quantities to retail, commercial, institutional or other professional businesses at a discounted price. The price you charge is typically two times the cost you incurred to manufacture the product for wholesale..

In my experience, I have found it much easier to sell my candles wholesale rather than retail. Both have huge benefits for different reasons. When selling wholesale you're able to get your products in various retail outlets without the headache of retail promotion. All wholesale orders are pre-paid prior to shipping out the orders.

Chapter 17: Resources

We have searched the web extensively to find the best candle suppliers on the market. Many of the companies listed below are ones we have purchased products from on occasion and the others are ones we use regularly. Although there are a ton of companies out there to choose from, I will only list the suppliers we have worked closely with or have heard good things about. The descriptions are provided from their websites.

RECOMMENDED WEBSITES

ALIBABA
www.alibaba.com

Alibaba.com Limited (HKSE: 1688) is the world's leading B2B [business to business] e-commerce company. They connect millions of buyers and suppliers from around the world every day through three marketplaces: an English-language marketplace (alibaba.com) for global importers and exporters, a Chinese-language marketplace (alibaba.com.cn) for domestic trade in China, and, through a joint venture, a Japanese-language marketplace (alibaba.co.jp) facilitating trade to and from Japan.
(HKSE: 1688 is Hong Kong's Exchanges and Clearing Limited)

ABOUT.COM
www.about.com

This website is an online neighborhood of hundreds of helpful experts, eager to share their wealth of knowledge with visitors.

THOMAS NET
www.thomasnet.com

This website offers a complete range of Internet marketing solutions to help industrial suppliers stand out from the competition and achieve their business goals.

The below websites are good sites to begin selling your products through:

eBay
www.ebay.com

eBay is the world's largest online marketplace—where practically anyone can sell practically anything at any time. It's an idea that Business Week once called "nothing less than a virtual, self-regulating global economy."

ETSY
www.etsy.com

Etsy is an online marketplace for buying and selling all things handmade.

ART FIRE
www.artfire.com

Art Fire is your free interactive community and handmade marketplace designed for artisans and crafters of all types.

BUSINESS RESOURCE WEBSITES

U.S. SMALL BUSINESS ADMINISTRATION
www.sba.gov

The SBA offers a wealth of information and guidance for entrepreneurs looking to start a business. Check out the website for free online courses, and for local resources to increase your business knowledge and productivity.

ENTREPRENEUR
www.entrepreneur.com
www.womenentrepreneur.com

Entrepreneur magazine offers a lot of information for the novice to professional business owner. The website offers a lot of information from business start up and marketing resources to networking with other likeminded business persons. Listen up ladies; they have created a website for you!

BETTER MANAGEMENT
www.bettermanagement.com

This company provides a wealth of information, articles, webcasts and other educational resources in improving the leadership and decision-making skills of businesses.

NEWSLETTER & MARKETING RESOURCES

BRONTO
www.bronto.com

CLICKZ
www.clickz.com

CONSTANT CONTACT
www.constantcontact.com

DIRECT MAG
www.directmag.com

EMAIL UNIVERSE
www.emailuniverse.com

GET RESPONSE
www.getresponse.com

INTELLI CONTACT
www.intellicontact.com

MAIL CHIMP
www.mailchimp.com

MARKETING TIPS

www.marketingtips.com

VERTICAL RESPONSE
www.verticalresponse.com

PUBLIC & PRESS RELATIONS RESOURCES

EZINE ARTICLES
www.ezinearticles.com

Expert Authors and Writers are able to post their articles to be featured within the site.

Our searchable database of hundreds of thousands of quality original articles allows email

newsletter publishers hungry for fresh content to find articles that they can use for

inclusion within their next newsletter.

PAY PER INTERVIEW PUBLICITY
www.publicity.com

Kocina Marketing Companies are populated with talented professionals whose sole

purpose is to help you reach your customers and teach them to buy your products.

PRESS RELEASE NEWSWIRE
www.prweb.com

PRWeb was founded in 1997 to help small businesses leverage the Internet to

communicate their news to the public.

PRESS RELEASE WRITING
www.press-release-writing.com

Press-Release-Writing.com can distribute your press release to the targeted channel(s) of

your choice, including top daily and national newspapers, top industry and segment

publications, TV, Radio, and top online news sources.

WORD FEEDER
www.wordfeeder.com

Copywriting and marketing for print media and the web.

BLOGS & NETWORKING WEBSITES

BLOGGER
www.blogger.com

Blog away about your business and all that you're doing in it.

TWITTER
www.twitter.com

Twitter is a service for friends, family, and co–workers to communicate and stay

connected through the exchange of quick, frequent answers to one simple question: *What*

are you doing?

MEETUP
www.meetup.com

Network in real-time with people all over the word; join groups of interest.

FACEBOOK
www.facebook.com

Network with people from your past to your present all over the world; join and create

groups.

TOAD FIRE
www.toadfire.com

TYPE PAD
www.typepad.com

WORD PRESS
www.wordpress.com

Create your own blog.

TRADE AND PROFESSIONAL ASSOCIATIONS, GUILDS AND ORGANIZATIONS

There are many associations out there to provide information about the candle industry from the USA to Canada to Latin America.

ALAFAVE
http://www.alafave.org/

The Latin American Candle Manufacturers Association–ALAFAVE–was created in 1999 as a non-profit association by a group of candle manufacturers and suppliers to the candle industry.

CANADIAN CRAFT & HOBBY ASSOCIATION
55 Macewan Park Road N.W.
Calgary, AB, T3K 3G1
Tel: (403) 770-1023
Fax: (403) 668-9166
Email: info@cdncraft.org
Website: http://www.cdncraft.org/

The Canadian Craft & Hobby Association fosters industry awareness, interests, growth and prosperity by developing and implementing first-rate programs, events and activities.

Financial savings, business and professional development, hands-on education, improved techniques and product training, timely news, trends and information, new profitable ideas, great industry exposure, promotional tools, networking and new friends. Each CCHA member has a voice. The rewards are outstanding.

CRAFTMASTER NEWS
PO Box 39429
Downey, CA 90239
Toll Free: (800) 871-2341
Tel: (562) 869-5882
Fax: (562) 904-0546
http://craftmasternews.com/

They list thousands of events, including street fairs, festivals, boutiques, home and garden shows, consignment malls and stores, farmers markets, city events and more... Currently they cover the following states: AZ, CA, CO, ID, KS, MT, ND, NE, NM, NV, OK, OR, SD, TX, UT, WA and WY. They're constantly in touch with promoters to provide the readers with the most accurate, current and complete listings of events available. Subscription cost annually is $48.95.

INTERNATIONAL GUILD OF CANDLE ARTISANS
http://www.igca.net/

Organization focused on educating the members and public on the standards of candle making.

NATIONAL CANDLE ASSOCIATION
1156 15th Street NW, Suite 900,
Washington, DC 20005
Telephone: (202) 393-2210
Fax: (202) 331-2714
Email: info@candles.org
http://www.candles.org/

The National Candle Association (NCA) is the major trade association representing U.S. candle manufacturers and their suppliers.

NATIONAL CRAFT ASSOCIATION
2012 Ridge Road East #120
Rochester, NY 14622-2434
Toll Free: 800-715-9594
Fax: 585-785-3231
Email: nca@craftassoc.com
Website: www.craftassoc.com

NCA is an information and resource center for the Professional Arts & Crafts Industry.

THE CRAFTS REPORT
N7450 Aanstad Rd
PO Box 5000
Iola, WI 54945-5000
Telephone 800-331-0038
Tel: 715-445-5000
FAX: 715-445-4053
http://www.craftsreport.com/

AROMATHERAPY ASSOCIATIONS

U.S.

American Alliance of Aromatherapy
P.O. Box 309
Depoe Bay, OR 97341

Institute of Aromatherapy
3108 Route 10 West
Denville, New Jersey 07834

International Aromatherapy and Herb Association
3541 W. Acapulco Ln.
Phoenix, AZ 85053
Website: http://aztec.asu.edu/makingscents/

National Association for Holistic Aromatherapy
4509 Interlake Ave N., #233
Seattle, WA 98103-6773
Website: www.naha.org

Aromatherapy Registration Council
Professional Testing Corporation,
1350 Broadway 17th floor
New York, NY 10018
Website: www.aromatherapycouncil.org

International

CANADA

Alberta Association of Professional Aromatherapists
21 Martingrove Way NE
Calgary, AB T3J 2T5
Website: www.albertaaromatherapy.org

British Columbia Alliance of Aromatherapy
Website: www.bcaoa.org

British Columbia Association of Practicing Aromatherapists
Website: www.bcapa.org

Canadian Federation of Aromatherapists
#103-1200 Centre St.
Thornhill, ON L4J 3M9 Canada
Website: www.cfacanada.com

AUSTRALIA

International Federation of Aromatherapists , Australia
PO Box 786
Templestowe, VIC 3106, Australia
Website: http://www.ifa.org.au

JAPAN

Aroma Environment Association of Japan
3-2-11-5F Kyobashi, Chuo-ku
Tokyo, 104-0031, Japan
Website: www.aromatherapy.gr.jp

KOREA

Korean Aromatherapy Association
3rd fl. Gapstar B/D
213-23 Nonhyun Dong Kangnam Ku
Seoul, Korea.

NEW ZEALAND

New Zealand Register of Holistic Aromatherapists
PO Box 18-399, Glen Innes
Auckland 6, New Zealand

SOUTH AFRICA

Association of Aromatherapists Southern Africa
PO Box 23924
Claremont 7735, Republic of South Africa

UNITED KINGDOM

Association of Medical Aromatherapists
11 Park Circus, Glasgow, G3 6AX
Website: www.complementarymedicinecentre.co.uk

Aromatherapy & Allied Practitioner's Association
PO Box 36248, London
Website: www.aromatherapyuk.net

Aromatherapy Organisations Council
PO Box 19834, London, SE25 6WF, UK
Tel: (440) 208-251-791
Website: www.aocuk.net/

International Federation of Aromatherapists, UK
182 Chiswick High Road
London, W4 1PP, UK

International Federation of Professional Aromatherapists
Admin Office, 82 Ashby Road
Hinckley Leics, LE10 1SN, UK
Website: www.ifparoma.org

Below is a list of web and graphic designers I have either worked with, observed their work, or continue to do business with. These are designers I highly recommend and are affordable for small business owners.

DEZIGNS BY T
366 East Stardust Drive
Pueblo, CO 81007-1630
Toll Free: 888-651-2153
Fax: 480-393-4542
Email: info@dezignsbyt.com
Website: www.dezignsbyt.com

Tanya Stesen is one of the head designers of the company and she has been my designer

for the last five years. Her work is outstanding! She has been only one of few designers I

have worked with who understands what I want and continues to make it happen.

FLYEYE DESIGN
Email: flyeye@flyeyedesign.com
Website: www.flyeyedesign.com

Jill Harner is the owner of this company and she has done work for my business. I'm

quite pleased with her work, as well.

JILL LYNN DESIGN
400 17th St NW Unit 1335
Atlanta, GA 30363 USA
Phone: 770-313-9363
Fax: 404-601-4850
Email: jill@jilllynndesign.com
Website: www.jilllynndesign.com

Founded in 2002 by solo-creative Jill Anderson, Jill Lynn Design creates sleek and lively

designs for books, packaging, and branding in print and on the web.

Below is a list of technical forums you can visit to find answers for many of your soy candle problems, a thorough list of fragrances that work well in soy wax, and to network with others doing what you do every day:

CANDLE TECH
www.craftserver.com/forums

MOON GLOW SOY CHAT
http://groups.yahoo.com/group/MoonGlowSoy/join

THE CANDLE CAULDRON
www.candlecauldron.com

CANDLE SOYLUTIONS
www.candlesoylutions.com

SOY WAX CANDLES.ORG
www.forumcityusa.com/index.php?mforum=soywaxcandles

JUST SCENT MESSAGE BOARD
www.justscent.com/board

THE SCENT REVIEW
www.thescentreview.com/board

WAHM (Work At Home Mom)
www.wahm.com

Chapter 18: Suppliers

WAX SUPPLIERS

BITTER CREEK CANDLE SUPPLY NORTH

42212 County Hwy. E
Ashland, WI 54806
Phone: (877) 635-8929
Fax: (715) 278-3904
E-mail: info@candlesupply.com
Web Site: www.candlesupply.com

I have been ordering from this company for the last seven years. I started out ordering

from this company when I was making gel candles but when I switched over to soy this

was the first company I ordered from. They offered the EZ Soy wax…I have to say that it

took me four months to realize that this wax was not the best for me but there are other

chandlers who have had better results.

CANDLE SCIENCE

2320 Presidential Drive, Suite 103
Durham, North Carolina 27703
Phone: 1-888-266-3916
Fax: 1-919-224-4930
E-mail: support@candlescience.com
Web Site: www.candlescience.com

I absolutely love this company! The entire staff–Dan, Michael and Diane–have always

been so helpful! They provide the best customer service ever. For me, that is far more

important than the products themselves. If you ever have any questions, feel free to

contact Mike and his awesome staff. This company offers an excellent turn time. I have

generally received my order within two business days.

CANDLE WIC COMPANY
3765 Old Easton Road
Doylestown, Pennsylvania 18902
Phone: 800-368-3352
Local: 215-230-3601
Fax: 215-230-3606
E-mail: info@candlewic.com
Web Site: www.candlewic.com

Candle Wic offers an extensive line of products from wax, herbs, fragrance oils, and

dyes, to molds, glassware, and additives. I usually purchase a few of my fragrances from

this company. I absolutely love the customer service I always receive.

POLYGON CORPORATION
1 Westinghouse Plaza
Boston, MA 02136
Phone: 617-268-4455
E-mail: polygonwax@aol.com
Web Site: www.polygonwax.com

Polygon carries a wide selection of waxes such as soy, gel, paraffin and beeswax.

GLASS CONTAINERS

FILLMORE CONTAINER
2316 Norman Road
Lancaster, PA 17601
Toll Free: 1-866-FILL-JAR (866-345-5527)
Phone: 717-397-4131
Fax: 717-509-3339
Website: www.fillmorecontainer.com

Fillmore Container's background is obviously in containers–they represent almost

exclusively USA-made glass container and closure manufacturers. They carry what is largely considered the most consistent out-of-the-box soy wax (NatureWax C-3) and all their TruScent fragrances have been developed or tested specifically for use in soy wax.

I personally have been ordering from this company for several years and have not been disappointed with the customer service or quality of products. Products have always been delivered in a timely manner. Fillmore Container is one of the top two companies I order my glassware from.

THE JAR STORE
221 South Street, Building F-5
New Britain, CT 06051
Phone: 860-826-1881
Fax: 860-826-1880
Web Site: www.jarstore.com

This company is a supplier of candle jars. We primarily order our jars from here. I have found The Jar Store prices are very competitive compared to other companies. I highly recommend ordering from here. Paula usually takes my orders and she's an absolute sweetheart.

RIEKES GLASS

Toll Free: 800-927-9989
Fax: 909-464-0877
E-mail: sales.order@riekesglass.com
Website: www.riekesglass.com

Riekes Distributing Company has been serving industry and retailers for more than fifty years. They offer a full line of glass products featuring Libbey Glass and other manufacturers in Europe, South America and Asia. They are a family-owned business that has sales in each of the fifty states, South America, Canada, the Caribbean Islands and the Middle East.

This company will send complimentary samples of containers for you test.

SKS BOTTLE & PACKAGING, INC.
2600 5th Avenue, Building 60 West
Watervliet, NY 12189
Phone: 518-880-6980
Fax: 518-880-6990
Web Site: www.sks-bottle.com

SKS is a supplier, consultant and designer of plastic bottles, glass bottles, plastic jars, glass jars, metal containers and closures for your packaging needs. Their online selection of containers and closures is extensive and priced right so you are getting the best selection of products at the best prices.

SPECIALTY BOTTLE
200 4th Avenue S
Seattle, WA 98108
Phone: 206-340-0459
Fax: 206-903-0785
E-mail: service@specialtybottle.com
Web Site: www.specialtybottle.com

Here's another company that specializes in candle jars, bath and body bottles as well as travel tins. This company is ideal for those who live on the West Coast to save on shipping. There are no minimum ordering requirements and their prices are competitive.

YES SUPPLY COMPANY
145 Whiley Road SW
Lancaster, OH 43130
Toll Free: 866-687-9385
Phone: 740-687-9385
Fax: 740-652-9089
E-mail: yessupplyco@yessupply.com
Website: www.yessupplyco.com

This company offers first quality glass products at wholesale pricing. Very prompt in

shipping.

PACKAGING SUPPLIES

FETPAK, INC.
70 Austin Blvd.
Commack, NY 11725
Phone: 1-800-883-3872
E-mail: fetpak@fetpak.com
Web Site: www.fetpak.com

Fetpak, Inc. is the leading distributor in the packaging supply business. They carry a wide

selection of gift bags, gift boxes, tissue paper, plastic bags, labels, tags, etc.

NASHVILLE WRAPS
242 Molly Walton Drive
Henderson, TN 37075
Phone: 800-547-9727
E-mail: info@nashvillewraps.com
Web Site: www.nashvillewraps.com

Nashville Wraps offers wholesale gift packaging. Minimum order is $25. Orders under $50 carry up to a $5 service charge. A nominal handling charge is added to all orders. Fast and prompt service!

SUNSHINE CONTAINER
New Jersey
Phone: 973-676-4432
Fax: 973-676-7392
E-mail: carton2000@cs.com
Web Site: www.sunshinecontainer.com

This company carries acetate containers for votive, tarts, and tea light candles, boxes for pillar or jar candles, display boxes, thank you bags and packaging boxes. We have used their acetate votive and tea light containers and I love them. It's all about presentation.

ULINE
2105 S. Lakeside Dr.
Waukegan, IL 60085
Toll Free: 800-958-5463
Fax: 800-295-5571
E-mail: customer.service@uline.com
Website: www.uline.com

Uline is the leading distributor of shipping, industrial, and packing materials to businesses throughout North America. They have warehouses in Duluth, GA, Breinigsville, PA, Waukegan, IL, Eagan, MN, Coppell, TX, Ontario, CA, Brampton, Ontario and Tijuana, B.C. Mexico.

VICTORY PACKAGING
Phone: 888-261-1268
Web Site: www.victorypackaging.com

Victory Packaging is a full-service packaging solutions company that has mastered both

the science and art of packaging. They are experts at the various aspects of packaging

design, creation, delivery, storage and management, and uniquely skilled in making those

components part of a comprehensive program that saves customers money and delivers

superior service. Minimum order is $250.

FRAGRANCE & ESSENTIAL OILS

BRAMBLE BERRY, Inc.
2138 Humboldt Street
Wellington, WA 98225
Toll Free: 877-627-7883
Phone: 360-734-8278
Fax: 360-752-0992
Web Site: www.brambleberry.com

Bramble Berry is a primary supplier of soap making supplies, but this company also

carries a high quality of candle fragrance oils, herbs, dyes and essential oils.

CANDLE WIC

3765 Old Easton Road
Doylestown, Pennsylvania 18902
Toll-Free:800-368-3352
Local: 215-230-3601
Fax: 215-230-3606
E-mail: info@candlewic.com
Web Site: www.candlewic.com

The Candlewic Company, like many companies, truly started as a hobby for Bill and Betty Binder back in the early 1970s. The Candlewic Company now has two locations in beautiful Bucks County, Pennsylvania and continues to lead the candle industry in new developments to make candle making easier and interesting for companies of all sizes. The Candlewic Company has focused 100% on candle making and is committed to serving all of their customers. The second generation Binders is now at the helm of Candlewic and continues to search for and offer new products.

JUST SCENTS

110 Water Street
Jackson, OH 45640
Phone: 740-286-3600
E-mail: customerservice@justscent.com
Web Site: www.justscent.com

Just Scents is owned by Becky Jo and is a supplier of highly fragrant oils. I have been quite impressed with the quality of this company's fragrances. A lot of the fragrances have an *excellent* scent throw in soy wax.

NATURAL SOURCING, LLC (FROM NATURE WITH LOVE)
341 Christian Street
Oxford, CT 06478
Toll Free: 800-520-2060
Phone: 203-267-6061
Fax: 203-267-6065
E-mail: info@fromnaturewithlove.com
Web Site: www.fromnaturewithlove.com

FromNatureWithLove.com (FNWL) has been a leader in supplying high quality

ingredients to the skin care, aromatherapy, spa and craft industries since 1997. FNWL

also offers a large selection of packaging supplies, bath accessories and equipment.

NATURES GARDEN CANDLES
42109 State Route 18
Wellington, OH 44090
Toll Free: 866-647-2368
E-mail: info@naturesgardencandles.com
Web Site: www.naturesgardencandles.com

Natures Garden Candles offer a pretty extensive list of supplies from candle making to

soap making. In my opinion, the fragrances have been a hit or miss in soy candles. They

offer great customer service and prompt shipping.

RAINBOW MEADOW
4494 Brooklyn Road
Jackson, MI 49201
Toll Free: 800-207-4047
Phone: 517-764-9765
Fax 517-764-9766
Website: www.rainbowmeadows.com

This company offers high quality pure essential oils. I have tested many of their oils in

soy wax and received very good results. Customer service is great! They always have prompt delivery.

SUNROSE AROMATIC
1120 Dean Avenue
Bronx, NY 10465
Phone: 718-794-0391
Fax: 718-792-3276
E-mail: support@sunrosearomatics.com
Web Site: www.sunrosearomatics.com

Sunrise Aromatics is the fulfillment of a lifelong dream acted upon by one very dedicated

individual, Rosanne Tartar. Rosanne founded Sunrise in 1997 as her part-time

pleasurable interest of many years, and when it metamorphosed into a full-time passion,

her business blossomed.

THE SCENTED NEST
Phone: 217-345-5013
E-mail: birds@scentednest.com
Website: www.scentednest.com or www.soycandlesuppliers.com

This company caters specifically to soy candle makers. They supply everything from

fragrance and a small selection of essential oils, to soy wax, wicks and so much more. I

have tried a few of their fragrance oils and was not disappointed! The fragrance oils are

slightly expensive but you pay for quality.

CIERRA CANDLES
4750 Longley Lane #103
Reno, NV 85902-5981
Toll Free: 800-281-4337
Local: 775-851-7022
Fax: 775-829-0111
E-mail: sales@cierracandles.com or info@cierracandles.com
Website: www.cierracandles.com

This company offers a complete line of products for candle making. They offer

competitive pricing and prompt shipping.

CANDLE CHEM
56 Intervale Street
Brockton, MA 02302
Phone: 508-586-1880
Fax: 508-586-1784
E-mail: info@candlechem.com
Website: www.candlechem.com

This company carries a complete line of high quality candle making supplies.

LONE STAR CANDLE SUPPLY, INC.
5800 Park Vista Circle
Keller, TX 76248
Phone: 817-741-0876
Fax: 817-741-0879
Website: www.lonestarcandlesupply.com

Lone Star Candle Supply serves candle makers all across the country by offering a large

selection of high quality candle making supplies. They stock everything needed for

you to produce beautiful, highly scented candles.

MILL CREEK SOY WAX CANDLE SUPPLY
Phone: 574-653-2098
Fax: 574-653-9036
E-mail: sales@millcreeksoycandlesupply.com
Website: www.mcsoywax.com

This company carries everything you will need to make beautiful soy candles and even

soy bath and body products.

MOON GLOW CANDLE & BODY CARE SUPPLIES
510 Heritage Drive
Unit 4
Spearfish, SD 57783
Phone: 605-717-1470
Fax: 605-717-1472
E-mail: info@moonglowcandles.net
Website: www.moonglowcandles.net

This company carries a complete line of candle making supplies, Millennium soy wax,

and soy-based fragrance oils.

PEAK CANDLE MAKING SUPPLIES
5455 W. 59th Avenue, Unit R
Arvada, CO 80003
Toll Free: 866-878-5181
Website: www.peakcandle.com

Peak Candle Making Supplies offers candle making supplies, soap making supplies,

fragrance oils, and starter kits, all at wholesale prices.

CANWAX
6315 Shawson Drive, Unit #6
Mississauga, ON L5T 1J2
Toll Free: 877-670-6002
Phone: 905-670-6002
E-mail: info@canwax.com
Website: www.canwax.com

Suppliers of candle supplies located in Ontario, this company offers classes and will ship

products to the U.S. No minimum order.

VILLAGE CRAFT & CANDLE
166 Queen street East
St. Marys, Ontario N4X 1B5
Phone: 1-877-668-6603
Fax: 519-284-9966
E-mail: info@vccandle.com
Website: www.villagecraftandcandle.com

This company carries a wide array of candle supplies, as well as offering candle making

classes. Lots of great things offered.

VOYAGEUR SOAP & CANDLE COMPANY
19257 Enterprise Way, Unit 14
Surrey, British Columbia, Canada V3S 6J8
Toll Free: 800-758-7773
Phone: 604-530-8979
Fax: 604-530-8978
E-mail: sales@voyageursoapandcandle.com / service@voyageursoapandcandle.com
Website: www.voyageursoapandcandle.com

Voyageur Soap and Candle specializes in supplies and packaging for all types of candle

making, soap making, bath, health and beauty care products.

SHIPPING RESOURCES

DHL
www.dhl.com

FEDEX
www.fedex.com

UPS
www.ups.com

USPS
www.usps.com

About the Author

JAMEEL D. NOLAN started making soy candles in 1998 and has not stopped. In 2004, she opened an e-commerce candle business. Ms. Nolan continued to develop her candle making talents to include having worked with all wax mediums such as paraffin, gel, palm and soy waxes. In addition to manufacturing her candles for businesses throughout the United States and selling retail through her website, Jameel assists new candle crafters in learning how to make soy candles the easy way and how to avoid the costly mistakes she made early on.

Thank you for your continued support!

Visit us online at:

www.ultimateguidetosoycandlemaking.com

Testimonials

"This is by far the *best* information out there on soy candle making. Most sources out there will give you some information but hold back on you knowing 'everything.' This book tells you everything you would need to know.

"I currently have a retail/wholesale business and wanted to extend it with a soy candle line. Because of running my current business, I did not have the many hours it would take to research making quality soy candle making. This book of information was invaluable. The information in it enabled me to purchase supplies and go right to making candles. By following the steps provided, I was able to make fewer costly mistakes and get answers to questions. I am currently doing many burn tests (great info on that as well) and getting my soy candle line ready to introduce with my existing products.

"Thank you for sharing such valuable information." *J. Theriot of Spring, TX*

"Your e-book is excellent! Very informative and professionally done. After all my years of teaching, very few books give detailed information the way yours does. I will be putting it on my website and referring to it in my classes." *J. Morais of Fairfield, CA*

"I bought your e-book, and so far I love it. As soon as it downloaded I started reading because it has been nothing here but trial and error, error and more error. Thanks so much for all of your help; I really appreciate it. I will be sure to let you know how things work out with following your advice. I started trying to make my own candles for the same reasons you did but have found it to be much more difficult than I first imagined." *B. Murphy of Pennsylvania*

"I purchased the *Ultimate Guide to Soy Candles* when I started to make candles for my massage business. I wanted something clean to burn in my office, as well as wanting to offer candles to my clients. Before buying the Guide, I just went online and found random instructions. I purchased wax, wicks, and containers, essential oils, and other scents. I quickly learned that candle making is an art with many variables.

"Nothing I tried seemed to be the correct combination of materials. So, after hair pulling and much frustration, I went back online to do more searches for better instructions. I found your site and your guide. With nothing to lose, I purchased the *Ultimate Guide to Soy Candles* and started again. The instructions are right on and easy to understand. The information included is priceless, as far as I am concerned. You cover all the problem areas in candle making and offer solutions. It has cut out so much trial and error, and I am thankful. I repurchased different wax and wicks, and now my candles burn correctly. The resources for material purchases are also valuable. Not only have I saved time, I believe I have saved money using the resources you included in the Guide. I am extremely happy with the vendors I have used and have experienced great product and fantastic customer service. I would recommend your book to anyone getting started in the art of candle making. Thank you!" *C. Marshall of Idaho*

"I read your opening page and I thought about myself. How many times I have stopped and started again because of fear, and I am an older person than you. I have always found some excuse for me to stop. Reading your story has regenerated my spirit to move on. I have had so many careers that I could have succeeded at many times over, if only I believed in myself. So I truly thank you for your inspiring story. I still have a full-time stressful job that, with God's help and my determination, I am looking forward to leaving in a year. Much success and many blessings in all your undertakings." *Rachel*

"I simply love your 1st eBook. I took every piece of advice and tip you wrote and I had wonderful results with making candles. I'm looking forward to the next e-book. Thank you. :)" *S. Edwards of Michigan*

"I recently purchased your book on soy candle making and started my own business in Pennsylvania. I want to thank you for the information, it was very timely, as I was struggling with what to purchase, from where, and exactly some of the issues you had when starting out. THANK YOU!" *K. Kirschner of Pennsylvania*

CPSIA information can be obtained at www.ICGtesting.com
Printed in the USA
LVOW090349250413

330731LV00001B/25/P